MICROSOFT WORD 2010
TIPS & TRICKS

YOU KNOW WORD...
BUT DO YOU REALLY *KNOW* WORD?

By Alicia Katz Pollock, MAT, MOS

COPYRIGHT

PREFACE

You know Word… but do you really *KNOW* Word???

This is not a book about how to use Word. Lots of people have already written about that.

This book is about how to thoroughly utilize Word. How to take advantage of everything it has to offer. How to bend it to your will. How to create with its tools and achieve exactly what you want. How to do what you already do… but in half the steps.

And, most of all, how to save your precious time.

If each of these tips & tricks shaves 3 seconds off your repetitive tasks, that's 11 minutes per day, or over 51 hours per year.

That's a week's vacation! And for $14.95, that's a cheap vacation.

Time is money. If you make $15/hr, you've also saved your boss $765 a year.

What are you waiting for? Let's get to really *KNOW* Word!

Love, Alicia ☺

DEDICATION

This book is dedicated to all my students who attended my classes and trainings through the years. It's been a joy to watch your faces glow, not just from the monitor, but from seeing your "AHA!" moments.

*"I've been recently deployed to Afghanistan, and had to update the Standard Operating Procedure manual for my section, which was in Word. Thanks to the skills I learned from your Word 2010 class, I was able to not only fix errors, but make it look great! The **"Find" and "Replace" buttons** were a Godsend. Thank you for showing me all the Tips & Tricks you did."*   *~Kris Baxter, Squad Leader*

This book is also dedicated to my delightful husband, Jamie, who supports all my wild endeavors with Grace and Zip. From restaurant-quality dinners; to taking care of business; to laughter, listening, music, and hugs, you really are a myth come to life.

Credits: Cover and Logo by Dustin Murdock

TABLE OF CONTENTS

ALICIA'S FAVORITE TIPS & TRICKS

Here are my very favorite Tips & Tricks to whet your appetite. As you read this book, you'll find dozens I left out!

CHAPTER 1: FILE MANAGEMENT

Word already saves your documents behind the scenes, but use these Tips & Tricks to take control of how it manages your files.

Recent Files

A document is never done, is it? It's rare that you finish with a file in one sitting. That's not a good idea anyway since it takes time and distance to proofread.

1. Reopen a Recent Document

To quickly get back to a recently opened file, **go to FILE→RECENT**. A list of the last files opened appears.

2. Change the Number of Files That Show on the List

To increase the number of files that appear on this menu, **click on the OPTIONS button** at the bottom of the sidebar, then **click on ADVANCED**.

Scroll down to the **DISPLAY section**. The first item says **SHOW THIS NUMBER OF RECENT DOCUMENTS**. Increase the number up to 50.

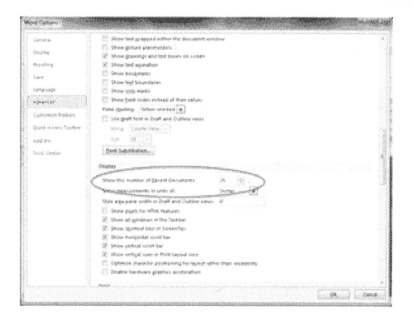

3. Quickly Access This Number of Documents

Click on the CHECKMARK at the bottom of the list, and type in a number. No matter what area of the FILE Tab you're on, you'll always see the most recent files.

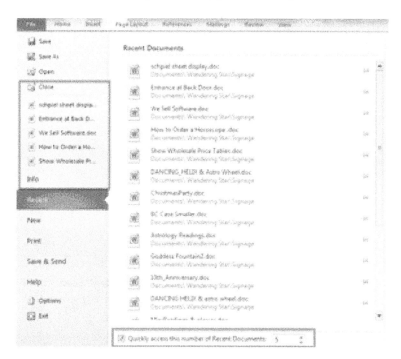

4. Pin Items to the Menu

For easy access to favorite files, even if you only use them occasionally, **click on the THUMBTACK** to the right of the item. The pushpin turns blue, and the item jumps to the top of the list. It will stay there indefinitely. To unpin the item, simply click the thumbtack again.

AutoSave Duration

Word automatically saves your document every 10 minutes in case of computer crash or power failure. But I can make a lot of changes in just a few minutes, so my advice: click Save every time you don't want to have to do a step twice. Or... set Word to AutoSave more frequently!

5. Set AutoRecover Duration

Go to the FILE TAB and click on OPTIONS at the bottom of the sidebar. **Click on the SAVE button**. Make sure there's a checkmark in front of **SAVE AUTORECOVER INFORMATION EVERY 10 MINUTES**. Then, **change the number** to a shorter duration. I use 2 minutes.

6. Make Sure to Keep Saved Versions

I also **keep a checkmark in front of KEEP THE LAST AUTOSAVED VERSION IF I CLOSE WITHOUT SAVING**. That way, if my computer crashes, when I open Word again, it asks me if I want to recover my file. I may still lose my very last changes, but at least I won't lose everything back to the last time I Saved.

7. Learn Where AutoRecover Files are Stored

I could change the **AUTORECOVER FILE LOCATION**, but Word is programmed to look there for backups. If I'm in a pinch and I need to open the file myself, I'll refer to this path to find the AutoRecovered file archive. If this is a constant issue for you, create a shortcut to this location in Windows Explorer to get to it quickly.

File Location

8. Default File Save Location

By default, when I save a file for the first time, Word tries to put it in my Documents folder.

That's a great start, but when I'm working on a project and constantly have to drill down into a subfolder, I tell Word to go straight there instead.

Go to the FILE Tab and click on OPTIONS at the bottom of the sidebar. **Click on the SAVE button.**

Where it says **DEFAULT FILE LOCATION, click the BROWSE button and use the dialog box** to select the new file location.

Now, when I do my first Save As for a new file, this folder becomes my default.

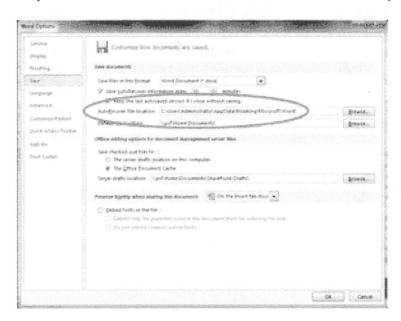

CHAPTER 2: INTERFACE

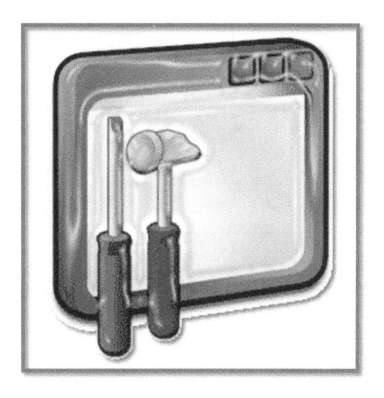

Modify Word's menus and tools to suit your workflow.

Opening Dialog Boxes

9. The Launcher Button

When MS Word 2007 first came out, the Ribbons were something of a shock to many people. Where were all the dialog boxes?

Never fear, they're still there! In the bottom right corner of each Group on the Ribbon is a tiny square with an arrow pointing out. When I click that innocent little button, Word's traditional dialog boxes open right up.

Modify the Ribbon

The Ribbon has replaced the Toolbars and Menus of old. All Word's commands are organized into tabbed strips. Similar commands are grouped together.

There's a little Launch button in the bottom right corner of some of the Groups so that you can access options that didn't fit on the ribbon.

Microsoft moved to this layout because, when they polled Word users about what features they wanted to see in the program, 90% of the suggestions were already in the software, but the commands were buried deep in menus.

Ribbons allowed Microsoft to pull features out of obscurity and make them readily available.

10. Expanding and Collapsing the Ribbon

That Ribbon does take up a lot of space, but I don't need to look at it all the time. To gain an extra inch of real estate on the screen, **double-click on a TAB, or press CTRL-F1.** It collapses so that all I see are the Tabs, and not the commands.

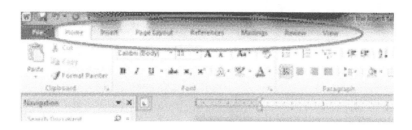

To use a collapsed Ribbon, **click on a Tab**, and it drops down. After choosing a command, the Ribbon closes again automatically.

To bring the Ribbon back, **double-click on a TAB again**.

Two more ways to expand and collapse the Ribbon are to **use the little ^** next to the Help question mark, and **right-click on the RIBBON and choose MINIMIZE THE RIBBON.** Both do the same thing.

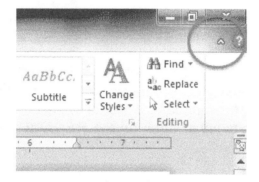

11. Modify Existing Ribbons

I like to add frequently used Commands to an existing Ribbon. But if you share a computer with other people, don't confuse them!

To modify the Ribbons, **click on the FILE Tab and then click OPTIONS** at the bottom. I can also get there by **right-clicking anywhere on the RIBBON and choosing CUSTOMIZE THE RIBBON**.

In the OPTIONS pane, click on CUSTOMIZE RIBBON in the left column. I now see two columns: the left contains the commands, and the right contains the Tabs.

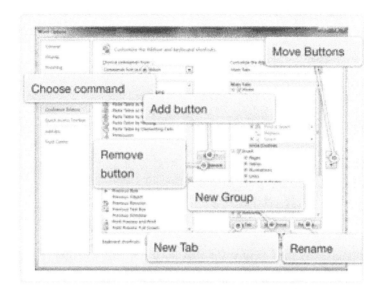

To add a command to an existing ribbon, I first have to create a new Group. I can't add a button to existing arrangements.

In the right column, I **click on the RIBBON I want to modify**. I **click the + SIGNS** to expand each out to see its Groups. At the bottom of the right column, **click the NEW GROUP button.** A new Group appears. If it's not in the correct location, **use the UP AND DOWN ARROWS** to move it. **Click on the RENAME... button** to give it a new designation.

Next, we'll add our Commands. At the top of the left column is a drop-down that says Popular Commands. I can change this to Commands Not in the Ribbon, or a subset of commands.

I'll **Click on the command I want**, and then on the **ADD>> button** to add it to my new Group. I'll continue in this way to gather my personalized commands.

If a command has no associated icon, a **GREEN BALL** appears. **Use the RENAME button to choose a custom icon for it**.

If I need to Remove a command or Group, **Click on it and Click on the <<REMOVE button**.

12. Create Your Own Tabs

I also like to add new Tabs to the ribbons to gather all my personal tools into one place.

Click on the NEW TAB button at the bottom of the right column. A **GROUP** is created automatically. **RENAME both of them.**

After that, the procedure is the same as before.

The Quick Access Toolbar

The Quick Access Toolbar appears in the upper left corner of all of the MS Office applications. By default, it has little buttons to manage the application window size, save a file, undo, and redo. But I like to customize it to contain my most commonly used commands so that they're available no matter what ribbon I'm on.

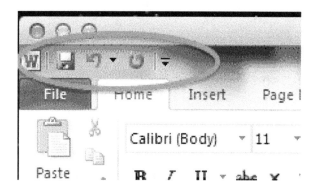

The buttons appear in the order I add them. I can reorder them, but by planning ahead, I customize the Quick Access Toolbar so it's organized from the get-go.

13. Change Its Location

When I've included a lot of commands, they may cover my document file name. So instead of the top corner, sometimes I move it underneath my ribbon.

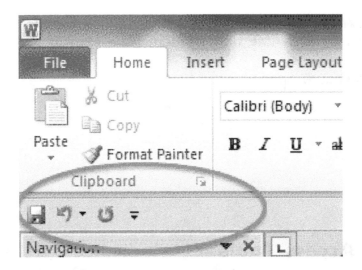

Click on the QUICK ACCESS TOOLBAR DROP-DOWN ARROW, then click on **SHOW BELOW THE RIBBON.** This does take up an additional row of screen space, but that location can sometimes work better. To put it back, **click the DROP-DOWN again and change it to SHOW ABOVE THE RIBBON.**

14. Add Frequently-Used Buttons to It

Click on the DROP-DOWN again, and **choose one of the most popular commands**. It now appears to the right of Redo. This is a great place to put a Quick Print or Email button!

To remove a button, **click on it again** to uncheck it.

15. Add a Ribbon Button to It

I frequently add Ribbon commands to the Quick Access Toolbar. **Right-click on any button and select ADD TO QUICK ACCESS TOOLBAR**. Now, no matter what Ribbon I'm on, I can get to the command instantly.

To remove a button, **right-click on it in the Quick Access Toolbar and choose REMOVE FROM QUICK ACCESS TOOLBAR**.

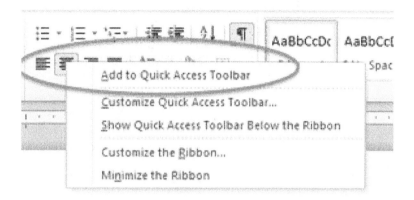

16. Add Any Command to It

I can also add any command in Word, even if it's not on a Ribbon. **Click on the Quick Access Toolbar DROP-DOWN ARROW and choose MORE COMMANDS**. This takes me into Word's Options, into a special Quick Access Toolbar area just for this purpose.

This procedure works just like Customizing the Ribbon, but I don't need to create Groups!

To reset the Quick Access Toolbar back to its default, use the **RESET BUTTON** down at the bottom.

17. Rearrange the Buttons on it

To reorder the Quick Access Toolbar, **click on the command to move, then use the UP AND DOWN ARROWS on the far right** to move it higher or lower on the list.

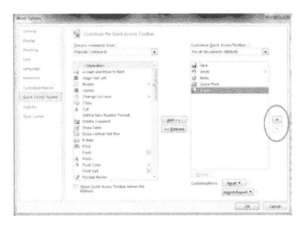

18. Apply the New Settings to Other Computers

To duplicate this Quick Access Toolbar setup on another computer, use the **IMPORT/EXPORT button** at bottom right to **Export all customizations**, which can then be imported into another machine.

The Status Bar

19. Modifying the Status Bar

The Status Bar is the gray bar across the bottom of the Word window.

On the left, it shows the number of pages in the document and the total number of words. It also has a button to run the Spell Checker.

On the far right, I can switch the views and magnify the screen, since I want to avoid squinting and craning my neck!

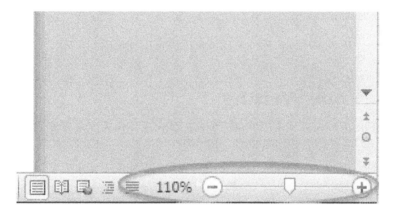

Click on PAGE: X OF Y, and the Find/Replace/Go To window opens. **Click on WORDS:** and see a full word count analysis.

But that's not all it can do, not by a long shot!

Right-click on the STATUS BAR and a long list of options appear. **Click on ANY**, and they are added to the bar.

Notice that some are already checked by default, but don't show up on the bar. They only appear when the context is right. For example, I won't see anything about Permissions appear until I actually lock down the document.

Some, like Line Number, are purely for reference, to give me information about my document. Others, like Spelling and Grammar Check or Overtype, are tools I can click to initiate.

Zoom in on Your Writing

When my eyes get tired, I like to enlarge my text without jeopardizing my layout.
Zoom features are found in several places around Word.

20. The Zoom Slider

In the bottom right corner of the window there's a slider. **Drag from left to right** to
enlarge the text. I also **click on the — AND + SIGNS**. The line in the middle is 100%.

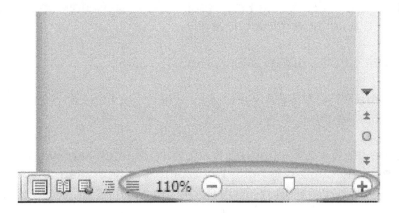

21. The Zoom Button

Immediately to the left of the slider it says 100%. **Click on the NUMBER**, and a Zoom dialog box opens. **Click on the DOT in front of any of the PRESETS**, or **change the PERCENT BOX**.

PAGE WIDTH expands the document to fill the screen from left to right.

TEXT WIDTH goes even farther, spreading the text from left to right. Scroll from left to right to see the margins.

WHOLE PAGE zooms out to see the entire page all at once. This is handy for looking at document aesthetics and fixing layout issues.

MANY PAGES shows multiple pages at a time. Click on the picture of the monitor, then on the grid of 8 pages to select how many pages we want to see.

22. The View Tab

On the **VIEW TAB**, there's a **ZOOM GROUP**.

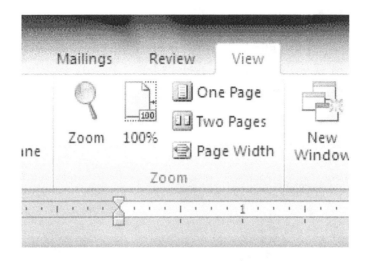

Click on the ZOOM button to bring up the same dialog box.

The **100% button** brings us back to the default view in one click.

ONE PAGE shows a whole page.

TWO PAGES shows two pages side-by-side.

PAGE WIDTH zooms in until the margins reach the edges of the window.

The Ruler

The Ruler is much more than a measuring stick across the top of the page and down the left side. It contains a variety of tools so that I can format my page layout without going into dialog boxes.

Note that when using the Ruler to adjust the layout, **changes only hold for the one paragraph the cursor is in**, and the next one after I press Enter at the end of the line.

Be sure to highlight several paragraphs or the entire document BEFORE using these steps.

23. Showing and Hiding the Ruler

Click on the TINY RULER ICON at the top of the vertical scroll bar to toggle the rulers on and off.

Go to the VIEW Tab and turn on the CHECKMARK in the SHOW group.

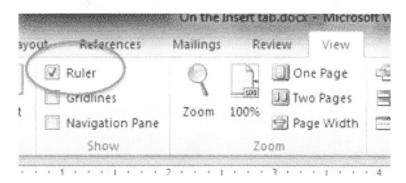

24. Changing Page Margins

Notice how the Ruler is white in the middle and blue over the page margins? If the text indent triangles aren't in the way, **hold the cursor over the line, and it turns into a DOUBLE-HEADED ARROW**. **Drag it left or right** to change the margins. It works the same way for the top and bottom margins on the vertical ruler.

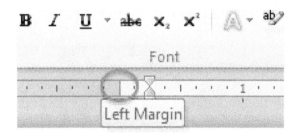

25. Working With Text Indent Markers

The triangles at the margins show the left and right text indents. Most of the time these are the same as the page margins, but when I make a block quote, I force the text to justify itself more narrowly than the rest of the page.

On the left side, the **BOTTOM SQUARE** is the left edge of the paragraph. This is the same as using the **INCREASE INDENT AND DECREASE INDENT buttons** on the Home Ribbon.

On the right side, the **TRIANGLE** is the right edge of the paragraph.

Drag either one of these and the paragraph margins adjust independently of the rest of the page.

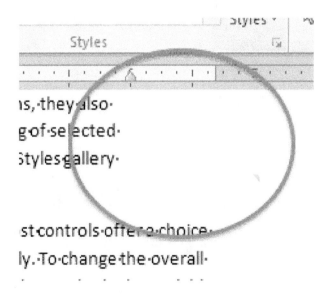

26. Setting First Line Indents

Look at the left margin markers in the Ruler. The top triangle is the First Line Indent, or the first line of the paragraph.

If I **drag the FIRST LINE INDENT TRIANGLE to the right**, it indents the first line of my paragraph. This is similar to pressing the Tab key on the keyboard to indent the first line, but it's actually "proper" word processing.

See **Paragraph Formatting** for other ways to set First Line Indents.

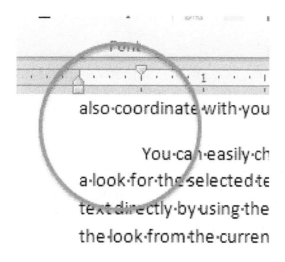

27. Setting Hanging Indents

The bottom triangle is the Hanging Indent, or the rest of the paragraph margin.

Drag the BOTTOM INDENT TRIANGLE to the right, and it indents the entire paragraph. Then **drag the top FIRST LINE INDENT TRIANGLE to the left** to make a Hanging Indent.

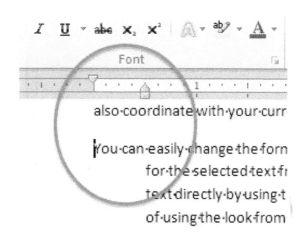

28. Setting Tabs

Tabs are covered in depth in a later chapter, where I show you how to set up the Ruler with left, center, and right Tab Stops.

Split the Screen

When I'm working on a long document, I sometimes need to refer to one page while working on another. I like to split the screen to view two different sections at the same time.

29. View Two Sections of the Same Document

There are several ways to split the screen. The first is a **TINY HANDLE** just above the Ruler icon above the vertical scroll bar. **I hold my cursor over it to get a DOUBLE-SIDED ARROW, then drag down.**

This allows me to scroll within the two sections independently.

I can also split the screen by going to the **VIEW Tab and clicking the SPLIT button** in the Window group (I can also **press ALT-CTRL-S**). **I click on the screen where I want the divider line.**

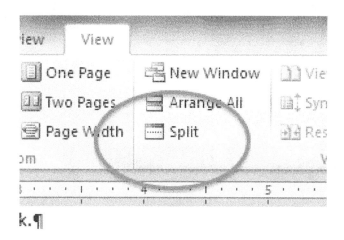

k.¶

When I'm done, that Split button now says **REMOVE SPLIT**. Usually, though, I simply **double-click on the LINE,** and it all goes away.

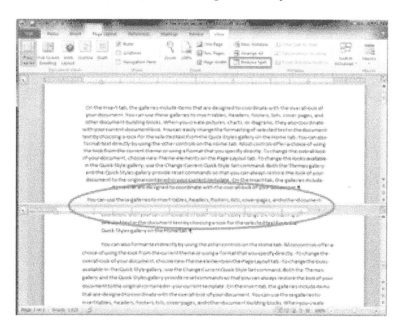

30. Show Two Documents Horizontally

To view two different documents at the same time, open them both. **Go to the VIEW Tab and click on ARRANGE ALL**. The two documents divide themselves horizontally across the top and bottom of the screen.

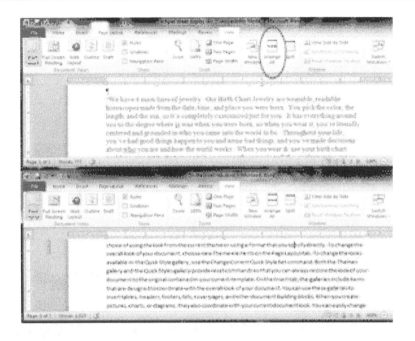

31. Show Two Documents Side-by-Side

Click on the VIEW SIDE-BY-SIDE button on the View Tab. The two documents arrange themselves in two columns.

Use the **SYNCHRONOUS SCROLLING button** for the two views to scroll simultaneously.

When the ribbons get narrow, these commands may be found on the **WINDOW drop-down**.

To return to normal view, **click on the RESET WINDOW POSITION button**. Or, simply maximize the windows again.

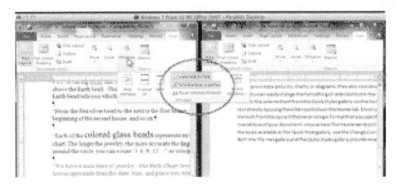

CHAPTER 3: KEYBOARD SHORTCUTS

It's easy to invoke all of Word's features from the Ribbons, but for speed and efficiency, nothing beats Keyboard Commands. There's a lot you can do without ever picking up your hands from the keyboard to reach for your mouse.

Commands Using the Keyboard

When I'm typing away, I like being able to choose commands from the Ribbon and dialog boxes so that I don't ever have to take my hands off the keyboard to reach for my mouse.

32. Using Keytips

To navigate the Ribbon using Keytips, **press the ALT key** on the left side of the keyboard. Or, **press the F10 key**. Little letters appear over each of the Tabs, and a 1-2-3-4-5 appears over the Quick Access Toolbar buttons. Some of the letters are the first letters of the Tab name. (Context-sensitive ribbons, the ones that appear when I click on a picture or a table, for example, always start with a J).

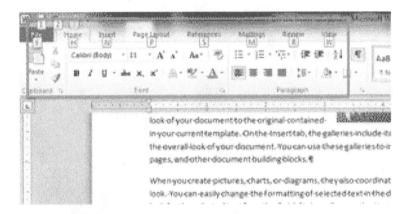

Next, I **press the letter(s) for the button I want**. For example, if I **press ALT-N then P**, I'll get a dialog box that inserts a picture from a file on my computer.

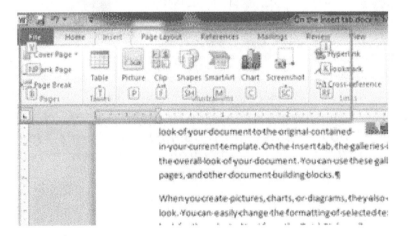

33. Using the Keyboard

Press ALT on the keyboard to activate the Ribbon. **Press the letter** of the desired Tab, or **use the LEFT AND RIGHT ARROWS** to switch from Tab to Tab.

Press the DOWN ARROW once on the keyboard to activate the command buttons.

Press the LEFT AND RIGHT ARROWS to move across the Ribbon to the desired button. **Press ENTER or SPACEBAR** to activate the command.

34. In a Dialog Box

In any dialog box, notice that many of the commands have little lines under one of the letters.

Hold down the ALT key and tap the letter to invoke that command.

Other dialog box tricks include **pressing the TAB key to move from option to option**. Also, **pressing ENTER is the same as clicking OK**.

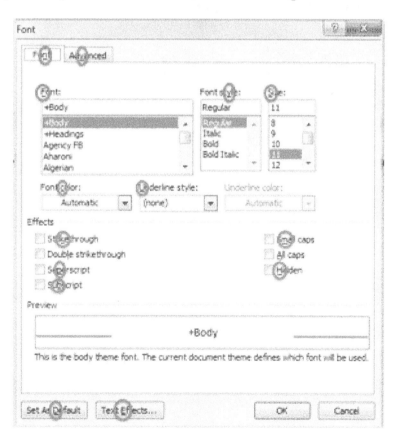

Keyboard Shortcuts

Power Users make good use of keyboard commands so they can work without having to take their hands off the keyboard and reach for the mouse.

35. How to Do a Keyboard Shortcut

CTRL ("Control") is the most common modifier key. **Hold down the modifier(s), then lightly tap the letter.** I don't push too hard or hold too long, or it'll perform the command several times!

Sometimes I need to add in or use additional keys, like **SHIFT** or **ALT**. **Shift** frequently does the opposite. For example, to move through a Table cell by cell, I press **Tab**. To move backwards, I also hold down the Shift key: **SHIFT-Tab**.

36. Common Shortcuts

Many of the basic functions are standardized across Microsoft Office, so most of the commands below work in Excel and PowerPoint as well.

Keyboard Combination	What it does
CTRL-N	new
CTRL-S	save
CTRL-Z	undo
CTRL-O	open a document
CTRL-P	print
CTRL-X	cut
CTRL-C	copy
CTRL-V	paste
CTRL-B	bold
CTRL-I	italic
CTRL-U	underline
SHIFT-F3	toggle capitalization (case)
CTRL-[	decrease font 1 pt
CTRL-]	increase font 1 pt
CTRL-SPACEBAR	clear formatting

37. Where to Find More Shortcuts

To find more keyboard shortcuts (there are hundreds!), either use Word's Help, or go to:

http://office.microsoft.com/en-us/word-help/keyboard-shortcuts-for-microsoft-word-HP010370109.aspx?CTT=1.

The keyboard shortcuts are categorized by topic. **Click on the + next to each category** to see a list of relevant suggestions.

At the very top of the list in the upper right, **click the SHOW ALL option** to see everything at once.

I keep this page bookmarked in my browser so I can look up keyboard commands any time.

Context-Sensitive Commands

38. Right-Clicking

Right-clicking the mouse on almost anything on my screen gives me a context-sensitive shortcut menu. This allows me to invoke frequently used commands without having to move my mouse very far around the screen.

What right-clicking does depends on what I click on. If I **right-click on the QUICK ACCESS TOOLBAR or RIBBON Tab a**, I get options to manage them. If I **right-click on a RIBBON BUTTON**, I get the option to add it to the Quick Access Toolbar.

If I **right-click directly on my TEXT**, I can:

1. Use the **MINI-TOOLBAR** to format my text
2. **CUT, COPY, AND PASTE**, and change my **PASTE OPTIONS**
3. Make changes to **FONT & PARAGRAPH FORMATTING, BULLETS & NUMBERING, STYLES, HYPERLINKS**, and more!

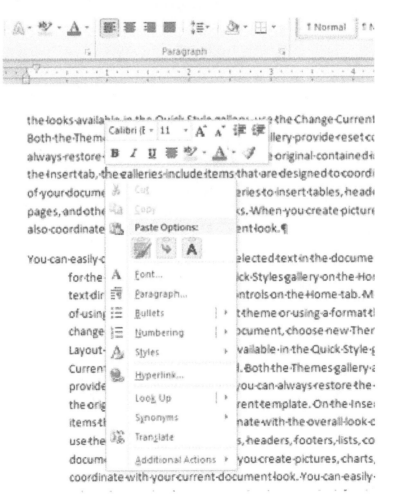

Right-click on the SCROLLBAR on the far right to jump to the top, the bottom, one screen's worth, and even **SCROLL HERE**, to move to that relative location in the document.

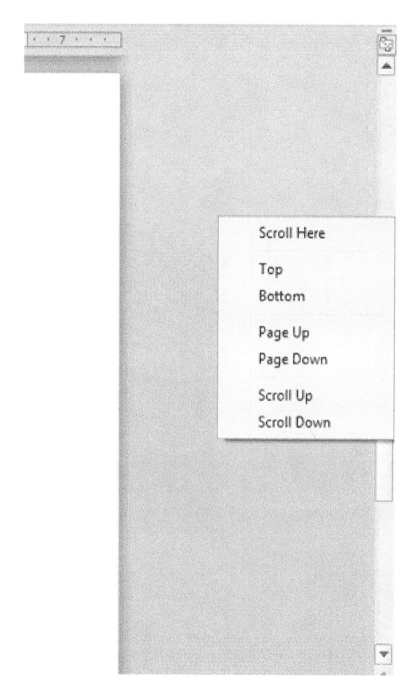

Right-click on OBJECTS like Tables, Pictures, Charts, or SmartArt for tools and options to manipulate them. Right-click **on the gray STATUS BAR** at the bottom of the window to add and delete tools.

Customize Status Bar	
Formatted Page Number	1
Section	1
✓ Page Number	1 of 2
Vertical Page Position	1.4"
Line Number	3
Column	33
✓ Word Count	1,023
✓ Number of Authors Editing	
✓ Spelling and Grammar Check	No Errors
✓ Language	
✓ Signatures	Off
✓ Information Management Policy	Off
✓ Permissions	Off
Track Changes	Off
Caps Lock	Off
Overtype	Insert
Selection Mode	
Macro Recording	Not Recording
✓ Upload Status	
✓ Document Updates Available	No
✓ View Shortcuts	
✓ Zoom	110%
✓ Zoom Slider	

F-Keys

39. Function Keys

Function Keys, also known as F-Keys, are the row of keys at the top of the keyboard. Word assigns them practical tasks, and more are available by using the **CTRL, SHIFT,** and **ALT** modifier keys.

Here are just a few useful F-Keys:

F1 — opens **HELP**

F4 — **REPEATS** my last action

F7 — runs the **SPELLING AND GRAMMAR CHECKER**

F9 — updates **FIELDS**, as in updating an existing Table of Contents

F12 — invokes **SAVE AS**

SHIFT-F1 — opens the **REVEAL FORMATTING PANE**

SHIFT-F3 — changes the **CASE OF LETTERS**

SHIFT-F5 — moves back to the **LAST CHANGE I MADE**

SHIFT-F7 — opens the **THESAURUS**

CTRL-F1 — opens the **PRINT PREVIEW window**

The table below is a sample from Microsoft's website. Read about the rest of the F-Keys at:

http://office.microsoft.com/en-us/word-help/keyboard-shortcuts-for-microsoft-word-HP010370109.aspx?CTT=1.

Function key reference

— Function keys

TO DO THIS	PRESS
Get Help or visit Microsoft Office.com.	F1
Move text or graphics.	F2
Repeat the last action.	F4
Choose the Go To command (**Home** tab).	F5
Go to the next pane or frame.	F6
Choose the **Spelling** command (**Review** tab).	F7
Extend a selection.	F8
Update the selected fields.	F9
Show KeyTips.	F10
Go to the next field.	F11
Choose the **Save As** command.	F12

CHAPTER 4: NAVIGATION TECHNIQUES

Ever find yourself scrolling around in a document trying to find a particular passage or phrase? Use these techniques to jump straight to your target content.

Navigating with the Keyboard

40. Using the Keyboard

I save myself a lot of clicking and scrolling by taking advantage of these Keyboard Shortcuts for navigating around my document.

Keyboard Combination	Where I move
Home	beginning of row
End	end of row
CTRL-Home	beginning of document
CTRL-End	end of document
Left & Right Arrows	one letter at a time
CTRL-Left Arrow CTRL-Right Arrow	one word at a time
Up & Down Arrows	one line at a time
CTRL-Up Arrow CTRL-Down Arrow	one paragraph at a time
Page Up Page Down	one screen at a time
CTRL-Page Up CTRL-Page Down	one page at a time

The Navigation Pane

The Navigation Pane is a tool that I use to move through my document quickly, in several different ways. To turn it on, **go to the VIEW Tab** and **put a CHECKMARK in front of NAVIGATION PANE**. Once it's open, I can browse my document by Headings, Thumbnails, and Search.

41. Browse by Heading

This technique requires labeling my sections using the Styles gallery, using the **Heading 1, Heading 2, and Heading 3 styles**. Once I've properly applied this organizational formatting, the **FIRST VIEW in the Navigation Pane** becomes a list of my sections and subsections.

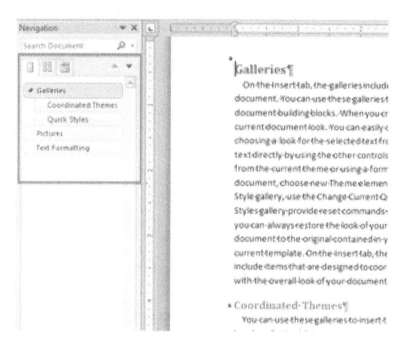

A tiny triangle appears in first-level headings that have subsections. **Click on the TRIANGLE to expand and collapse the list.** Second-level headings are slightly indented. It never ceases to amaze me how handy this is.

Click on the HEADINGS to jump to that section. **Use the UP AND DOWN ARROWS** to skip from section to section. **Click and drag the SECTION BARS** to rearrange the document. Much faster than cutting and pasting!

To instantly change between Heading 1, 2, or 3 styles, as well as change the section's indent, **right-click on a SECTION and choose PROMOTE or DEMOTE**.

42. Navigate by Thumbnail

Thumbnails show tiny previews of each page so that I can jump around by appearance.

Click on the SECOND Tab to see a picture of each page.

Click on the PREVIEWS to move around.

43. Locate Using Search

Click on the THIRD Tab for a SEARCH BOX.

When I **type in A WORD OR A PHRASE**, all occurrences become highlighted in yellow, and are listed in the Navigation Pane along with their context.

Click on EACH MATCH or use the UP AND DOWN ARROWS to visit each one.

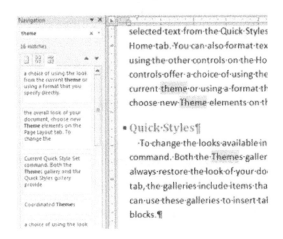

Browsing Your Document

44. Browse by Object

Ever wonder about that little circle in the bottom right corner, below the scrollbar? It's the Browse by Object button, and it gives me a powerful way of zipping through my document. I can jump from picture to picture, table to table, footnote to footnote, or to a particular location.

By default, the **DOUBLE ARROWS** above and below the circle jump up or down one full page at a time.

When I **click the CIRCLE or press CTRL-ALT-HOME**, a little window pops up asking how it should scan my document. **Choose the OBJECT TYPE.** Then, **use the UP AND DOWN ARROWS** to navigate.

Quick·Style·Set·command.·

mands·so·that·you·can·

your·current·template.·On·

e·with·the·overall·look·of·

ooters,·lists,·cover·p

,·or·diagrams,·they·

Browse by Page

230%

- **GO TO** opens a dialog box, where I can search for a specific Section, Line, Bookmark, Comment, and many other markers. **This box is covered extensively later in this chapter.**
- **FIND** opens up the **Find and Replace** dialog box.
- **EDITS** remembers the last 3 locations where I made changes.
- **HEADING** jumps between all my Heading 1, Heading 2, and Heading 3 Styles.
- **GRAPHIC** jumps from picture to picture.
- **TABLE** moves from table to table.
- **FIELD** moves between fields in a form.
- **ENDNOTE** jumps from endnote to endnote.
- **FOOTNOTE** jumps from footnote to footnote.
- **COMMENT** moves between reviewers' comments.
- **SECTION** takes me from section break to section break.
- **PAGE**, the default, navigates to the first line of each page.

Go To

The Go To dialog box is perhaps one of the most underutilized feature in Word. When I want to jump directly to a particular item in my document, I never waste time scrolling around looking for it.

45. Opening the Go To Dialog Box

There are several ways to get there:

- **Click on the HOME→FIND DROP-DOWN ARROW** on the far right and **choose GO TO....**
- **Start a FIND AND REPLACE**. Go To is on the third tab.
- **Click on the PAGE COUNT (PAGE: 1 OF 3) button** on the Status Bar in the bottom left corner of the window.
- **Click on the BROWSE BY OBJECT button.**
- **Press F5.**

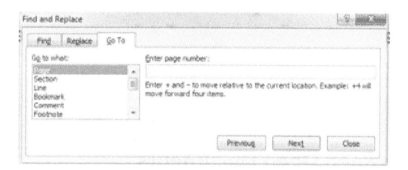

46. Choose Your Destination

The Go To dialog box gives me many of the same options as **BROWSE BY OBJECT**, plus a few more:

- **LINE** refers to the number of rows in my document.
- **EQUATION** jumps me from mathematical equation to equation.
- **OBJECT** gives me a list of anything I've pasted in from other Microsoft programs using **INSERT OBJECT**.

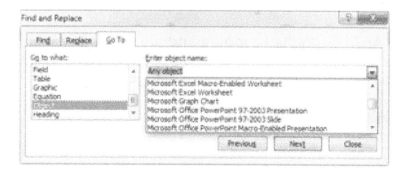

47. Enter the Item Number

Go To counts the quantity of what I've chosen. I can **enter the NUMBER for whichever I want to go to.** For example, if I know that I want to go to my 4th table, I **pick TABLE off the list, and type 4** in the box.

I can also move ahead or back a particular number of items. **Enter + or — before the number.** For example, if I want to jump ahead 3 tables, **enter +3** in the box.

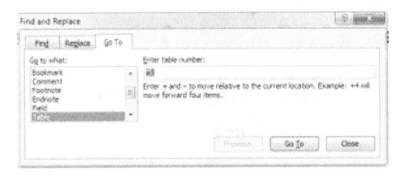

Switch Between Open Documents

It's common for me to work on two or more documents at once. Sometimes one is a reference; other times I'm multitasking.

Here are several ways I move back and forth between them.

48. Ctrl-F6

Press CTRL-F6 on the keyboard to toggle between Word's open windows.

49. Alt-Tab

Hold down the ALT key on the keyboard and tap the TAB key once (keep ALT down). An overlay appears with icons for all my open windows. **Continue to press TAB** until the desired document is highlighted. **Let go.**

Press SHIFT-TAB to go the other way.

If I just type **ALT-Tab, ALT-Tab,** I toggle between my two most recent windows.

50. The View Tab

Click on the VIEW TAB, then on SWITCH WINDOWS. I can **pick my document off the list.**

51. Using Windows

Depending on what version of Windows you're using, or your individual settings, this behavior may vary.

In earlier versions of Windows, there's at least one **ICON FOR EACH WORD DOCUMENT** on the task bar at the bottom of my screen.

Click on the CORRECT DOCUMENT to jump to it.

In more recent versions of Windows, you'll see **ONE WORD STACK ICON** with a number of open items.

Click on the STACK, and thumbnails of the open documents appear. **Click on the desired file.**

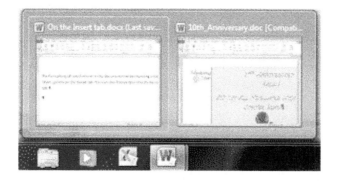

CHAPTER 5: SELECTION SHORTCUTS

Dragging across content to select it is second nature, but here are several techniques you can use to be more efficient.

Selecting Content for Formatting

Have you ever tried to highlight text by dragging, and your document starts running across your screen? Never again! Dragging across text to select it for formatting is natural, but that's just the beginning of the possibilities.

52. Drag From the End

When selecting text, always **start from the END and drag to the BEGINNING**. Usually I have more open space at the end, so my cursor is more forgiving. When I start at the beginning, I have to aim really carefully to click in the right place.

When selecting several lines of text, **drag UP OR DOWN before dragging LEFT AND RIGHT**. This helps the selection stop jumping around as I move.

53. Shift-Click

To highlight a large area, I start by **clicking my cursor once at the beginning** (don't hold down the button, just click). Then, I **use the scrollbar to move down to the end, hold down the SHIFT key, and click where I want the selection area to end**. The entire passage between the cursor's origin and last position highlight.

54. Jump to the Beginning or End of a Selection

If something is highlighted, I like to **press the LEFT OR RIGHT ARROW** on my keyboard, and my insertion point jumps right to the selection's beginning or end.

55. Selection Shortcuts

Here's how to highlight specific parts of a document:

Select what?	How to select
A word	double-click on it
A sentence	CTRL-click on it
A paragraph	triple-click on it
Entire document	CTRL-A, or Home→Select→Select All
A list	Click on the bullet or number
A table	hover the cursor over the table and Click on the + that appears in the upper left corner

56. Selecting Multiple Items

Hold down the CTRL key to select more than one non-contiguous item. For example, **select a word, then hold down the CTRL key and select another one**.

To select multiple objects, like pictures, hold down the SHIFT key and click on each one. If I make a mistake, I can SHIFT-click again to toggle it back off.

57. Using the Shift Key

By adding the SHIFT key, I can extend selected text. **If something is already highlighted, hold the SHIFT key down and click farther down.** The selection includes the new content.

Here are more Shift key tricks:

Keyboard Combination	What is selected
Shift-Home Shift-End	to the beginning or end of row
CTRL-Shift-Home CTRL-Shift-End	to the beginning or end of document
Shift-Left & Right Arrows	one letter at a time
CTRL-Shift-Left Arrow CTRL-Shift-Right Arrow	one word at a time
Shift-Up & Down Arrows	one line at a time
CTRL-Shift-Up Arrow CTRL-Shift-Down Arrow	to the beginning or end of paragraph
Shift-Page Up Shift-Page Down	one screen at a time

58. Fine-Tuning Selection Options

By default, when I drag, Word selects a whole word at a time. But personally, I like being able to select just the suffix to change the tense, and Word's tendency to select the entire word gets in my way.

To change this behavior, **go to FILE→OPTIONS→ADVANCED**, and look at the **Editing Options** section. **Uncheck WHEN SELECTING, AUTOMATICALLY SELECT ENTIRE WORD.**

Another consideration is that Word always includes the ¶ at the end of a paragraph. **Uncheck USE SMART PARAGRAPH SELECTION** to include just the text but not the final Enter.

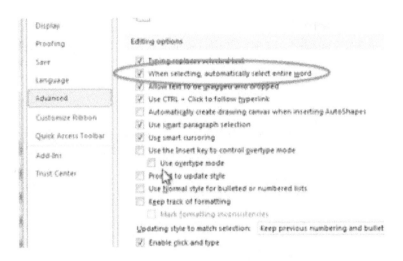

Selection Tools

59. The Selection Bar

The **SELECTION BAR** is an invisible toolbar in the left margin of every document. The only way to know it's there is to watch the cursor when it is to the left of the text. Notice that the cursor shape turns into an arrow pointing up and to the right?

This is one of my most efficient word processing tools.

While my arrow points at my text and I click my mouse, it selects one row (notice it's a *row*, not a sentence).

When I **CLICK AND DRAG downward,** I can **select several rows at once.**

When I **DOUBLE-CLICK,** I **select my entire paragraph.**

When I **TRIPLE-CLICK,** I **select my entire docu   ment.**

Text·Formatting¶

You·can·also·format·text·directly·by·usir
choice·of·using·the·look·from·the·current·theme
overall·look·of·your·document,·choose·new·The
available·in·the·Quick·Style·gallery,·use·the·Char
gallery·and·the·Quick·Styles·gallery·provide·rese
document·to·the·original·contained·in·your·curr
that·are·designed·to·coordinate·with·the·overal
insert·tables,·headers,·footers,·lists,·cover·page:
pictures,·charts,·or·diagrams,·they·also·coordin:
the·formatting·of·selected·text·in·the·document

Double·click

60. Using F8 to Select Text

Here's a great Function Key that very few people know — the F8 key is called "Extend Selection," and when I press it repeatedly, it highlights my content for me.

First, I **click in my text and press F8** to turn it on.

Press it again, and the **WORD** the cursor is touching becomes selected.

Press it a third time, and my **CURRENT SENTENCE** becomes selected.

Press it a fourth time, and my **ENTIRE PARAGRAPH** turns blue.

And when I **press it a fifth time**, my **ENTIRE DOCUMENT** is now ready for formatting.

CHAPTER 6: CREATING CONTENT

Here's a collection of Tips & Tricks you can use when you're typing content into your document.

Placeholder Text

61. Random Boilerplate Text

Sometimes I need several pages of text so that I can test a technique, give a demonstration, or create a placeholder for future content.

In fact, this technique is how I generated the sample document used to create the screenshots throughout this book!

The secret is to type in the document what looks like an Excel formula:

=rand(#,#)

"Rand" stands for "random." The first number is the number of paragraphs to create. The second is the number of sentences in each paragraph.

=rand(20,3)¶

So if I **type =Rand(20,3)** into a blank document, I get 20 paragraphs of 3 sentences each.

On a PC, the boilerplate text contains an explanation of Themes, Galleries, and Quick Styles.

On a Mac, "The quick brown fox jumped over the lazy dog" repeats over and over again.

Formatting Marks

It's much easier to see what's going on behind the scenes and fix formatting issues when I can see the hidden formatting characters.

It may seem distracting at first, but after awhile you won't be able to "see" your document without them! And don't worry, they don't print.

62. Show/Hide ¶

Turn on Show/Hide ¶ by **clicking on the button near the center of the HOME ribbon**, or **press CTRL-SHIFT-8** (I think of it as CTRL-*).

I love the little dots that appear between words, so I can see if I accidentally pressed the spacebar too many times.

There's a ¶ symbol in every place I had pressed Enter on my keyboard.

Tabs are denoted by a →.

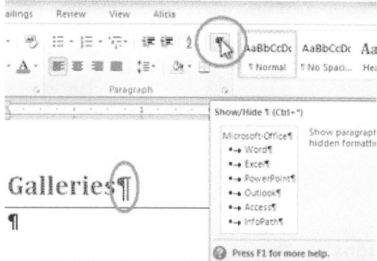

63. Always Show Formatting Marks

Sometimes I want to see certain formatting marks all the time, even if Show/Hide ¶ is off.

I go into FILE→OPTIONS→DISPLAY and check the symbols I always want to see.

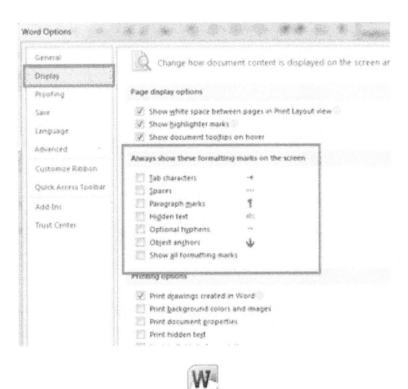

Paste Options

When I copy content from other sources, whether it be from another file, another program, or the web, it pastes into my document, but maintains its original formatting. Most of the time, it looks completely different, and then I have to manually reformat it to match my document.

Instead, I take advantage of Paste Options to bring in just the content, and leave the formatting behind.

64. Smart Tags

Immediately after pasting, a little yellow square with a clipboard appears in the lower right corner.

Click on it, or press the CTRL key to open it. Inside are three squares.

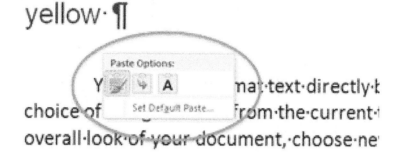

The first, **KEEP SOURCE FORMATTING**, maintains all the font and paragraph formatting from the original I copied.

The second, **MERGE FORMATTING**, keeps some of the paragraph formatting, but matches the font and size of the text around it.

The third button, **KEEP TEXT ONLY**, abandons all the original formatting and adopts the format of the destination text. This is the one I use most often.

Sometimes, there's a fourth button, **USE DESTINATION STYLES**. If I have styles defined in both documents, like Heading 1, but they're defined differently, the pasted content takes on the style definition of the target document, but the rest of the original formatting is maintained.

65. The Paste Button

The first button on the Home ribbon is Paste. It has two halves. The top half does a standard Paste. The bottom half gives the same options as the Smart Tag.

66. Paste Formatting Only

A neat trick I use allows me to duplicate just the formatting from the original source, without pasting the content.

Copy the content from the original source, highlight the target text in the active document, and press CTRL-SHIFT-V. This pastes the appearance, but not the text.

67. Setting the Paste Default

When I'm doing a lot of copying and pasting between documents, I usually need one of these Paste Options exclusively. Instead of changing the setting every time I paste, I like to set the default.

On either the Smart Tag or the Paste button drop-down, **choose SET DEFAULT PASTE**. This opens Word's **ADVANCED OPTIONS**, in the **CUT, COPY, AND PASTE** section.

Here I can define my default format for when I Paste or CTRL-V, and refine other behaviors. As I mentioned before, I personally keep this on **KEEP TEXT ONLY**.

I can even set different defaults for pasting within my document, between Word documents, or from other applications.

There are additional options in this window to fine-tune the behaviors to my specific needs.

Inserting Today's Date

When I add today's date, I don't need to type it — I can insert it all at once, as a field. Even better, I can change how it's formatted, and even have it update automatically every time I open the file, which is great for Templates.

68. Insert As I Type

As I type the date in my document, Tooltips appear that predict what I'm going to type. **Press Enter** to accept the suggestion. For example, as I start typing "Janu",

Word suggests "January," and I press Enter to insert it. If I **keep typing the rest of the date**, it may offer to autofill in the day and the year as well.

69. Insert Today's Date and Time

I **click on the document where I want to put the date. Go to the INSERT RIBBON, and choose DATE AND TIME** on the far right.

Select how the date should look. To always use this style, **click the SET AS DEFAULT button**.

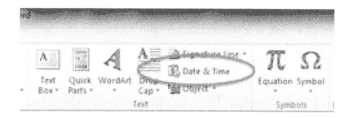

70. Update Automatically

If I use a document frequently, especially a Template, I **put a checkmark in front of UPDATE AUTOMATICALLY**. Every time I open the document, I see the current date. Be careful how you use this, though. If the document needs to show the actual date it was created, do NOT check this box!

71. Using a Keyboard Shortcut

I can also insert the date with the keystroke **ALT-SHIFT-D**. This inserts the date as a field — click on it to see the field container.

To change the format, use the instructions above to change the Default style, and reinsert the field.

The field maintains the original date. **Click on the UPDATE button to change it to today's date**.

72. Using Different Calendars

Right-click on a DATE FIELD and choose EDIT FIELD.... In the right column are options for **ISLAMIC, HINDU, AND THE SAUDI ARABIAN CALENDARS**.

There's a checkbox for using the same date format used the last time I clicked **INSERT→DATE AND TIME** from the Ribbon.

There's also a checkbox **PRESERVING FORMATTING DURING UPDATES**, so if I've made it bold and italic, I don't have to reapply formatting after forcing a date update.

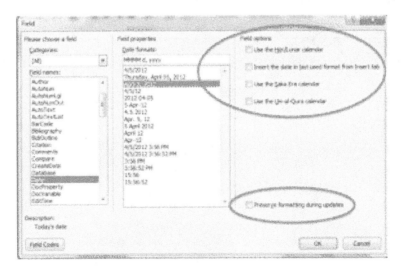

Automatic Formatting

73. Click-and-Type

Here's another one of my secret tricks!

Have you ever noticed that if you hold your cursor in the middle of an empty white area below your content, its shape changes to an I-beam with lines after it?

This is the click-and-type cursor.

To add new content below what you already have, **don't repeatedly press ENTER, TAB, OR CENTER**.

Instead, **point where you want to start, and DOUBLE-CLICK**.

The insertion point jumps to this new location, automatically inserting any paragraphs, tabs, and spaces it needs to get there.

Turn on the SHOW/HIDE ¶ BUTTON to see the newly created formatting.

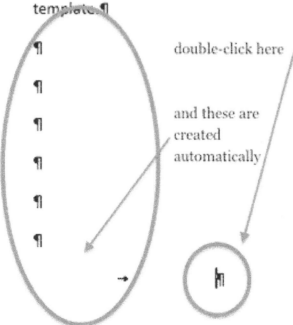

tab. To change the looks available in the Q
Set command. Both the Themes gallery an
that you can always restore the look of you
template.¶

double-click here

and these are
created
automatically

Overtype Mode

When replacing old content, most people just select it, delete it, and type in the new text. But sometimes I need to see the old content as I replace it.

To do that, I use Overtype Mode, and my insertion point moves over existing text as I type.

74. Set Up Overtype

Go to FILE→OPTIONS→ADVANCED and check off USE THE INSERT KEY TO CONTROL OVERTYPE MODE.

There's also an option to **check USE OVERTYPE MODE**, then Overtype is on by default. **I'll need to press INSERT to add text the way I do now**, when existing content gets pushed ahead. Thus, it is best to leave this unchecked.

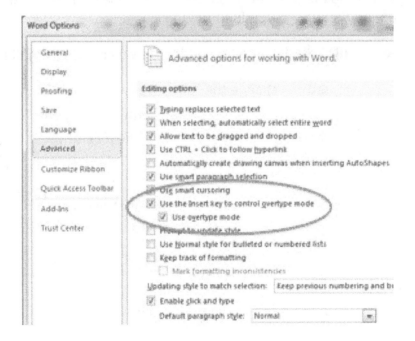

75. The Insert Key on Your Keyboard

Click at the beginning of text to be replaced. Tap the INSERT (or Ins) key on your extended keyboard (probably above Delete and next to Home).

Start typing, and the old content disappears under the cursor.

Just **be VERY careful to press INSERT again when ready to go back to adding new content**. I've seen people accidentally overwrite their entire document!

76. Overtype in the Status Bar

Right-click on the STATUS BAR and select OVERTYPE. A new button appears that says **INSERT. Click on it, and the mode toggles to OVERTYPE**. Now I'm in the mode that overwrites my content as I type.

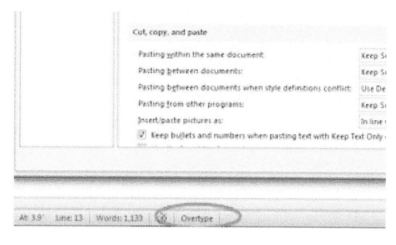

AutoCorrect and AutoFormat

Word's AutoCorrect, the feature that corrects my spelling as I work, has an added bonus — I frequently use it to update formatting, insert symbols, and even turn abbreviations into words.

AutoCorrect, AutoFormat, and Replace text as you type are all found under the **FILE →OPTIONS→PROOFING→AUTOCORRECT OPTIONS...** button.

77. Symbols and Faces

I use these symbols all the time in my document, and it's easier to type them than to use commands to create them.

Try this yourself in a blank document:

Type (c). It turns into ©. The same works for **(tm)** ™ and **(r)** ®.

:-) turns into ☺ and **:-(** into ☹. Other faces work as well.

<-- becomes ⬅, and <== turns into ⬅. There are additional arrows, too.

These symbols are found on the **AUTOCORRECT Tab UNDER AUTOCORRECT OPTIONS**.

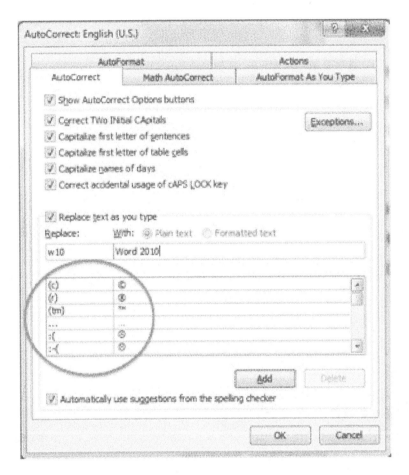

78. Replace Text as you type

I use AutoCorrect to create custom abbreviations for text I type constantly. Instead of typing "Word 2010" over and over again, I type w10, and it instantly expands. Some substitutions require me to type a space to trigger the replacement.

To create your own abbreviations, **go to FILE→OPTIONS→PROOFING. Click on the AUTOCORRECT OPTIONS button**.

In the **REPLACE BOX, type the abbreviation**.

In the **WITH BOX, I enter the full text I want to substitute**. Be very careful not to use abbreviations that occur in natural language, or they'll be triggered in the middle of the content. When in doubt, try a period or other character before the abbreviation (.w for Word).

There is no limit to the number of characters in the With text. I've even included entire paragraphs.

79. AutoFormat Punctuation

AutoFormat is what changes quotation marks, fractions, ordinals, and hyphens to proper formatting.

If I type a word--another word, after I press the spacebar at the end of the last word, the -- becomes an — (em-dash).

I like to use this technique to turn on Bullets by starting with an * followed by a space. When I start typing, the * becomes a genuine bullet and the list indents automatically.

To turn this behavior on or off, **go to the AUTOCORRECT PANE as described above. Look on the AUTOFORMAT Tab and the AUTOFORMAT AS YOU TYPE Tab**.

Why are there two panes that are so similar? No one is quite sure, but **the AUTOFORMAT Tab** waits for me to invoke the formatting manually, while the **AUTOFORMAT AS YOU TYPE Tab** works its magic automatically as I enter my content.

Symbols and Special Characters

Symbols refer to text shapes from degrees to ordinals to mathematical operands. Special Characters are dashes, special spaces, and other typological characters.

Both can be accessed through the Ribbon, keyboard shortcut, or using **AutoCorrect**.

80. Symbols

Click on the INSERT RIBBON→SYMBOL button on the far right. There are 20 frequently used symbols.

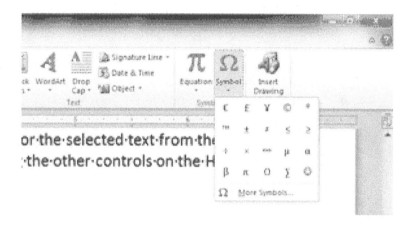

For more, **click on MORE SYMBOLS...** at the bottom.

In the Symbols dialog box, scroll up and down to see all the characters that come in the current font. **Try different fonts to see different symbols.** Try out Webdings and Wingdings for a vast collection of images.

To insert any symbol, **DOUBLE-CLICK on it**.

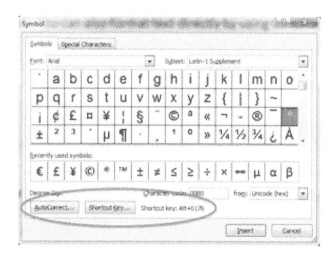

81. Special Characters

Click on the second Tab in the dialog box to see Special Characters. We've already talked about **dashes** and **copyrights** in the previous section, but take note of these additional features:

- A **NON-BREAKING SPACE** is a space that sticks two words together so they always stay on the same line. This is great for Company names.
- A **NON-BREAKING HYPHEN** does the same thing, but with a — instead of a space.
- A **PARAGRAPH** creates a printed ¶ mark.
- An **ELLIPSIS** turns four periods into an actual end of sentence….

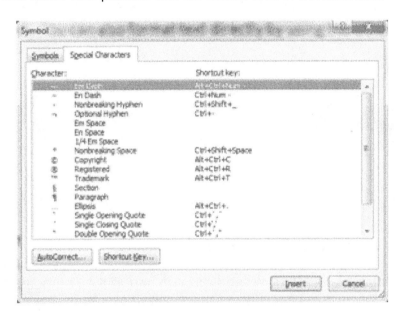

82. Keyboard Shortcuts

Many Symbols and Special Characters already have keyboard shortcuts assigned, but they can be changed.

Click on the SHORTCUT KEY... button to get a dialog box. Type the new keyboard combination that is easy to remember. Be careful not to assign a command that is already in use.

Assign that Keyboard Shortcut for use in the NORMAL.DOT TEMPLATE, making it available for all of Word, or **use the drop-down to change it to just this one document**.

Click on the AutoCorrect... button to assign an ABBREVIATION to the Symbol or Character.

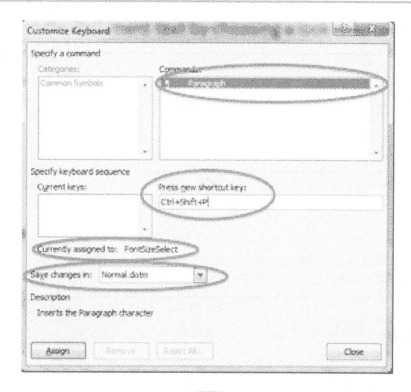

Horizontal Lines

One of my tricks with quite the "wow factor" is inserting artistic lines into my documents. To insert a horizontal line (also called a "horizontal rule"), there are three ways to do it.

83. AutoFormat

The first way is one of my obscure Word secrets. On a blank line, **type these 3 characters in a row and press ENTER.** A line appears across the page:

--- **HYPHENS** creates a thin line

_____

___ **UNDERSCORE** creates a thick line

═══

=== **EQUALS** creates a double line

═══

**NUMBER** makes a thin-thick-thin line

═══

*** ASTERISK makes a dotted line

~~~ TILDE makes a wavy line

84. Clip Art Lines

Word's built-in Clip Art Gallery contains dozens of images that act as lines. **Open up INSERT→CLIP ART, and search for LINES**. When I have an internet connection, I **INCLUDE OFFICE.COM CONTENT** for more choices.

Insert any of the images. If it doesn't extend across the page, **use any of the RESIZE HANDLES** to make it larger — but keep in mind that these are images, so if it's extended longer than its original dimension, it may become fuzzy.

As an added bonus, any of the features on the **PICTURE TOOLS→FORMAT Tab** can change the color, shadow, style, and effects of the line image.

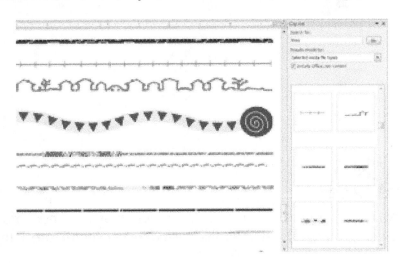

85. Bottom Borders

This technique works best on Headings.

Click in the paragraph of text you want a line under. Click on the HOME Tab→BORDERS button — Bottom Border is usually the default. This places a line across the page, underlining not just the text but the rest of the row, too.

Click on BORDERS AND SHADING, the last option on the drop-down list, **to refine the weight and color of this line**.

When I press Enter at the end of the paragraph, this border may extend down to the next row, an effect I don't want.

Use the CLEAR FORMATTING button on the HOME ribbon, and the border returns to the desired text.

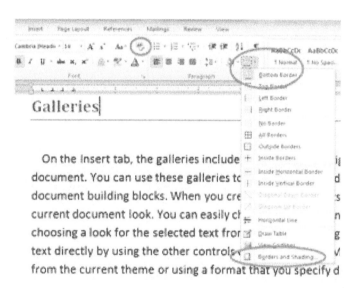

86. Shapes

Click on the INSERT RIBBON→ SHAPES button. On the drop-down gallery, the second section has a series of lines. Some have arrowheads; others have bends and angles.

Pick one.

Click where the line begins, and drag to where the line ends. To keep the line straight, **hold down the SHIFT key** while dragging.

Upon letting go, each line has a resize handle at the beginning and end to change the dimension. Lines that have curves and bends also have adjustment diamonds to refine the angles.

Use the DRAWING TOOLS→FORMAT ribbon to stylize the line's color and special effects.

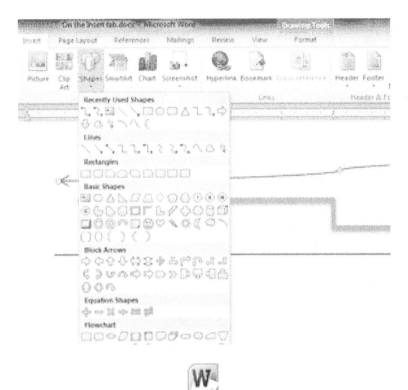

The Clipboard

When I'm transferring content from place to place, the last thing I want to do is copy/paste, copy/paste, copy/paste. By using the Clipboard, I can instead collect up to 24 items and then paste them all at once, instead of one at a time.

It even lets me copy between Office applications, from Word to PowerPoint or Excel.

87. Customizing the Clipboard

To control when the Clipboard appears and how it notifies you, **click the LAUNCHER BUTTON in the CLIPBOARD GROUP on the HOME Tab**. The Clipboard opens.

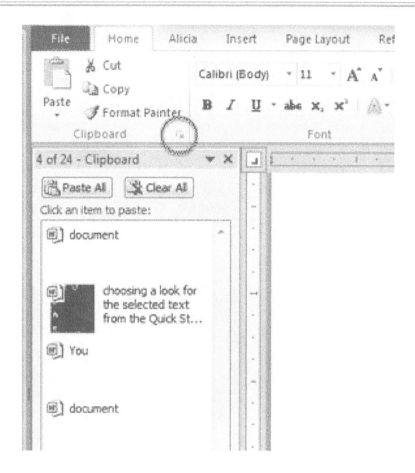

Click on the OPTIONS button at the very bottom. The first 3 options determine when I see the Clipboard:

- **SHOW OFFICE CLIPBOARD AUTOMATICALLY** opens the pane every time I Copy or press CTRL-C.
- The second choice **OPENS THE CLIPBOARD WHEN CTRL-C IS PRESSED TWICE**. I find this option most practical.
- I may want to **COLLECT WITHOUT SHOWING OFFICE CLIPBOARD**.

Normally, if the Clipboard isn't open, I can only paste the very last item, and the rest are forgotten. This option still stores all of my copying without showing me the list.

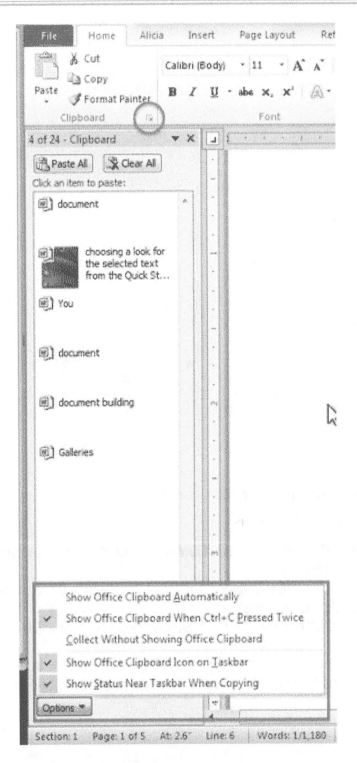

- **SHOW OFFICE CLIPBOARD ICON ON TASKBAR** presents a little yellow icon in the bottom right corner, in the status area of the Windows Taskbar. Double-Click on the Taskbar icon to open the Clipboard any time.
- **SHOW STATUS NEAR TASKBAR WHEN COPYING** pops up a yellow box in that same right bottom corner telling you how many of the 24 slots you've used up.

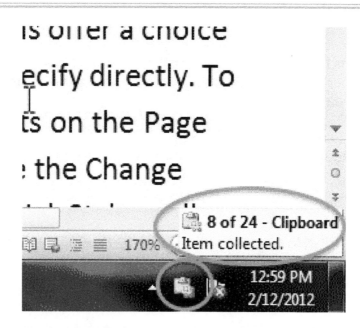

88. Gathering and Pasting Items

When the Clipboard is open, each item I copy is added to the list in reverse order, with the newest on top.

Click anywhere in the document, then on any one of these items, to paste it.

Continue by clicking on the next target destination, then on the next item in the Clipboard, for the next paste.

89. Paste All and Clear All

Use the PASTE ALL button to paste all the items all at once, in the order they were gathered.

Use CLEAR ALL to empty the Clipboard and start over again.

The Spike

The "Spike" takes its name from old-fashioned store receipts. When the cashier was done with a customer's order, they'd slap it onto a metal spike to store the receipt until the end of the day.

In Word, the Spike is much like the **Clipboard**, except it works with Cut items instead of Copied items.

90. Cut to the Spike

Instead of using CTRL-X to cut my content, I **use CTRL-F3**. The item is stored for pasting.

I then keep cutting until I have all my gathered items.

91. Paste the Spike

After I've cut out all of the items, I **click where I want to paste all, and press CTRL-SHIFT-F3.** All the items appear in the order I cut them, and the Spike is emptied.

If I don't want to clear the Spike, instead **type SPIKE and press F3**. The items paste, and are ready to be used again.

I can also **go to the INSERT RIBBON→QUICK PARTS→AUTOTEXT. Find SPIKE on the list, and click on it to paste the Spike**.

If Pasting the Spike is including the ¶ at the end of the item, and I need to turn off this behavior, **turn off Smart Paragraph Selection**.

92. See the Spike

To see what's on the Spike, **go to INSERT→QUICK PARTS→BUILDING BLOCKS ORGANIZER, and click on SPIKE** for a preview of the content.

Advanced Find and Replace

Find and Replace is one of my favorite power techniques. Not only does it allow me to substitute one word or phrase for another, but its advanced features really let me get creative with its use.

Do note, however, that it takes attention to detail when using this technique. After making big changes, scan the results carefully to make sure that no inadvertent changes were made. For example, when writing this book, I didn't turn on **Match Case** when I was trying to find the word "Click" at the beginning of a sentence, and capitalized every single instance of the word.

If you do make a mistake, **immediately UNDO**!

93. Opening Find and Replace
Opening Find:

- On the **HOME ribbon, click the FIND button on the far right or press CTRL-F**. This opens the **Navigation Pane**. If I select a word first, that word automatically appears in the Search box.
- **Click on the DROP-DOWN ARROW next to the FIND button on the HOME ribbon and choose ADVANCED FIND**. This opens up the Find dialog box.
- **Click on the PAGE: button on the Status Bar. Then click on the FIND Tab in the dialog box.**

Opening Replace:

- On the **HOME ribbon, click the REPLACE button on the far right, or press CTRL-H.** This opens the Replace dialog box. If I select a word first, that word automatically appears in the Find what: box.
- **Click on the PAGE: button on the Status Bar. Click on the REPLACE Tab in the dialog box.**

94. Finding and Replacing

To simply find a word or a phrase, it's easiest to **use the NAVIGATION PANE**. I also **use the FIND NEXT button in the dialog box** to skim through occurrences.

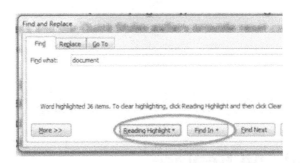

In the **Advanced Find dialog box, click on the READING HIGHLIGHT button, then HIGHLIGHT ALL** to put a yellow highlight around all instances of the word.

Use the FIND IN button to search a pre-selected segment, or choose MAIN DOCUMENT to search the whole file.

To repeat a find, press SHIFT-F4. To repeat Find after closing the Find & Replace window, press ALT+CTRL+Y.

When using Replace, either **REPLACE the word one at a time, or click REPLACE ALL to do all instances at once**.

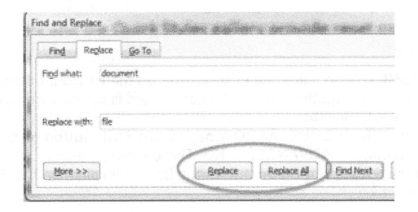

95. Search Options

Here's where the power lies—refine the Search parameters. **Click on the MORE>> button to see SEARCH OPTIONS**.

- The **SEARCH: DROP-DOWN** allows you to search upwards, downwards, or the whole document.
- **MATCH CASE** matches lowercase and capital letters.
- **FIND WHOLE WORDS ONLY** prevents partial letter matches. For example, if I tried to replace THE with A, if I didn't click this option, "theater" becomes "aater" and "then" becomes "an".
- **USE WILDCARDS** allows for partial matches. **Type the letters and use an * for the rest (Shift-8)**. For example, if I Use Wildcards for "typ*", it matches "type," "typing," and "typed."
- **SOUNDS LIKE** finds words that sound the same, like "to," "two," and "two."
- **FIND ALL WORD FORMS** locates all verb tenses. If I check this box and search for "choose," it also locates "choosing" and "chosen."
- **MATCH PREFIX AND SUFFIX** works in conjunction with the other options to only find matches that share the same beginning or ending.
- **IGNORE PUNCTUATION AND WHITESPACE** ignores differences in hyphens and spacing.

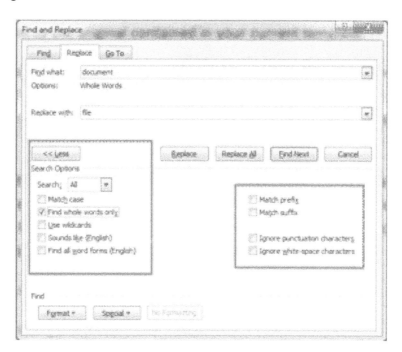

96. Find and Replace Formatting

And that's not all! I'm not limited to replacing content.

I can also use Find and Replace for formatting, including boldface, font color, paragraph formatting (like centering or line spacing), styles, and much more.

I could, for example, find all text that's bold and red, and replace it with blue italics. Or if I'd manually formatted section headers as 16-pt Bold Arial, I could replace them all at once with the Heading 1 style.

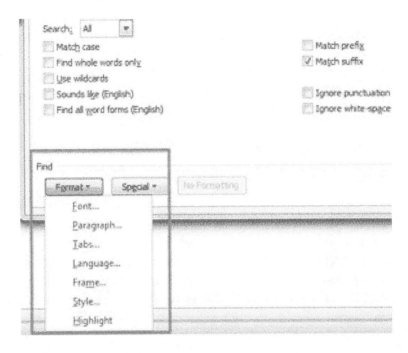

97. Find and Replace Special Characters

This is one of my moneymaking expert tricks. If a document was crafted using Enter to create an extra space between paragraphs, and the Tab key to indent paragraphs, I like to reformat the document using proper word processing techniques of **Paragraph Spacing** and **First Line Indent**.

Instead of having to go through my entire file deleting ¶ marks and tabs, I use Find and Replace Special Characters.

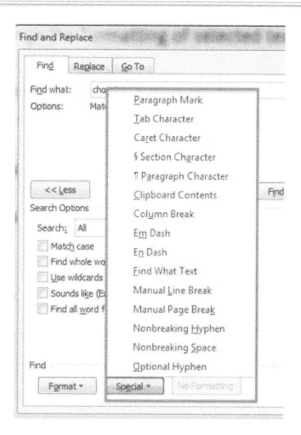

In the Find box, click the SPECIAL drop-down and choose PARAGRAPH twice, then TAB CHARACTER (it will show ^p^p^t).

In the REPLACE box, choose PARAGRAPH, then REPLACE ALL. The extra ¶ will disappear, as will the Tab.

Then the **Paragraph Spacing** and **First Line Indent** settings can take over.

There! Now you can put me out of business.

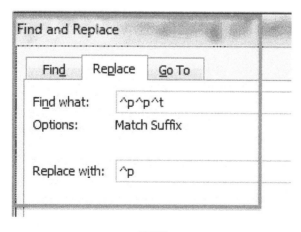

CHAPTER 7: FORMATTING TEXT

Arial

Arial Black

Comic Sans MS

Courier New

Georgia

Impact

Times New Roman

Trebuchet MS

Verdana

How you format text helps your reader understand complex ideas and the organization of your document. These advanced Tips & Tricks save time in formatting your text.

Reveal Formatting

Sometimes when I work with my formatting, it just won't behave. It leaves me confused, wondering exactly what I'm missing.

Instead of manually puzzling it out, Word's Reveal Formatting Pane shows me exactly what Word sees so that I can take control of character, paragraph, and page formatting.

98. The Reveal Formatting Pane
Click on or select any formatted text, and press SHIFT-F1.

A pane opens on the right side of the screen.

At the top is a Selected text box showing what text I'm looking into.

There are 3 main sections—Font, Paragraph, and Section—that can be expanded and collapsed using the + and - in their gray bars.

In each section are blue underlined categories, and indented underneath are the specifics for the text selection.

To make changes or fix problems with that formatting, **click on those BLUE UNDERLINED CATEGORIES to go to the dialog box where those options are set**.

99. Options

At the bottom of the list, **look for DISTINGUISH STYLE SOURCE**. This tells me if the formatting is part of an applied style, or something I applied directly.

100. Compare to Another Selection

Click on the FIRST text sample, put a checkmark in front of COMPARE TO ANOTHER SELECTION, and click in the SECOND sample.

The Formatting differences pane now shows both, the first and second separated by a ->.

Formatting Inconsistencies

When I have particular formatting applied to many items, I need to make sure that they're all exactly the same.

I turn on Mark Formatting Inconsistencies so that Word alerts me to slight differences as I type.

101. Mark Formatting Inconsistencies

Go to FILE→OPTIONS→ADVANCED, and put checkmarks in front of KEEP TRACK OF FORMATTING & MARK FORMATTING INCONSISTENCIES.

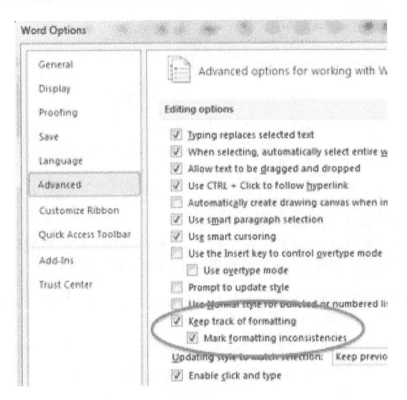

102. Find Errors on the Fly

As I work, Word analyzes my paragraph and character formatting, looking for slight differences. It looks for errors in list formatting, and times when I've replicated a style by directly applying formatting.

Such inconsistencies result in a blue underline.

Right-click on the BLUE UNDERLINE and choose to FIX the error, IGNORE IT ONCE, or IGNORE THE RULE EVERY TIME.

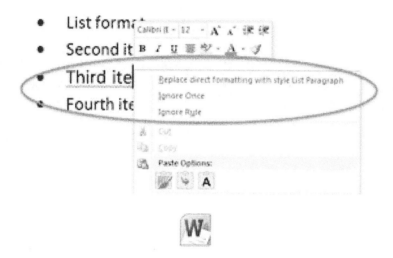

Theme Colors vs. Standard Colors

When I work with font colors in Word, there's a top grid of coordinated colors going from light to dark. These colors are part of the Theme applied to my document, and make it possible to change the look and feel of my document with just one click.

103. Theme Colors

Themes are chosen on the Page Layout ribbon. Every Theme comes with its own coordinated color set, a range of hues that work well together.

When applying Heading styles and other elements out of the Gallery, their default colors are defined by the document's Theme.

The default Theme is Office, and its main color scheme is blue.

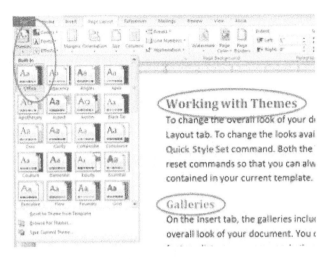

When I **choose a color shade from the THEME COLORS** and later switch to another theme, those colors change accordingly. In other words, what was once blue may turn green or orange.

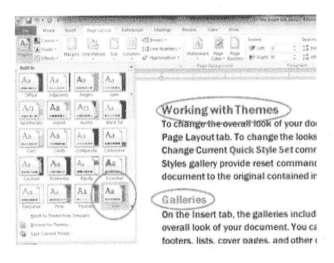

104. Standard Colors

If I **select a color from the STANDARD COLORS rainbow** at the bottom of the drop-down, that color stays the same no matter what Theme I choose.

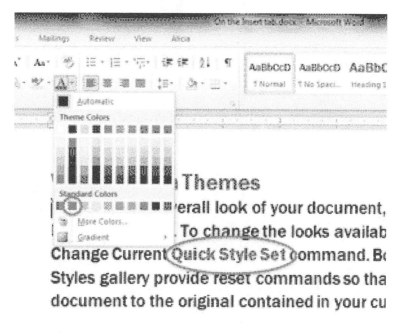

105. Creating Your Own Theme Colors

When I want to customize the colors and then use them again in another document, I create my own Theme Color set.

Go to the PAGE LAYOUT ribbon and select the COLORS drop-down.

Choose CREATE NEW THEME COLORS. In the dialog box, **click the drop-down for one of the six Accent Colors**, or the defined colors. **Click MORE COLORS...** at the bottom of the window.

Pick a new color—by staying in the same horizontal range, the color coordinates relatively well with the others in that set.

Save the new Theme with a new name, and it will be available for future documents as well.

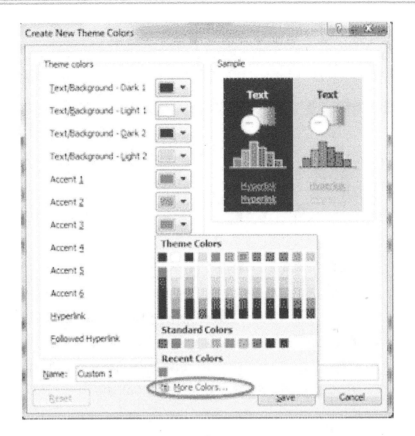

Using Hidden Text

Hidden Text is the perfect solution when I need to include text for my own reference that I don't want to print. I use it for instructions, dated material, or notes to myself.

106. Hidden Text

Select the text to hide. On the HOME ribbon, use the FONT group LAUNCH BUTTON to open the Font dialog box, or press CTRL-D. Use the CHECKMARK to format the text as HIDDEN.

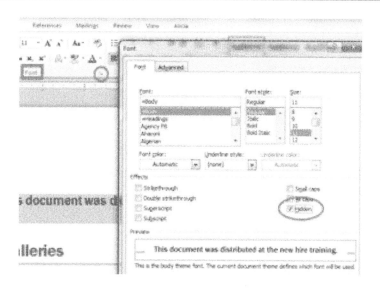

107. Hide and Show the Text

Use the SHOW/HIDE ¶ button on the HOME ribbon to toggle the visibility of the Hidden Text. When visible, there's a thin dotted line underneath.

To always show Hidden Text, even when formatting marks are off, **go to FILE→ OPTIONS→DISPLAY→ALWAYS SHOW THESE FORMATTING MARKS ON THE SCREEN, and put a check in front of HIDDEN TEXT.**

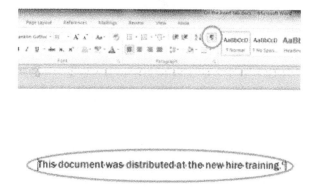

108. Print Hidden Text

By default, Hidden Text does not print. To print a document and include the Hidden Text, **go to FILE→OPTIONS→DISPLAY→PRINTING OPTIONS, and put a check in front of PRINT HIDDEN TEXT.**

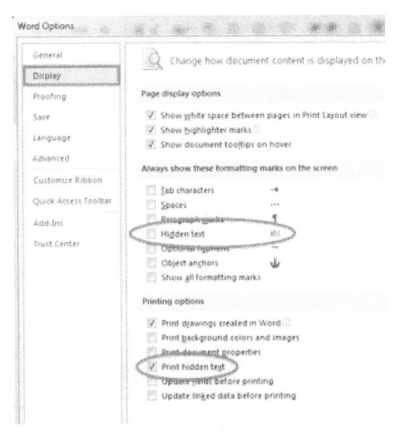

Non-Breaking Spaces and Hyphens

Non-breaking Spaces look like normal spaces between words, but they prevent a phrase from splitting in the middle. This is great for company names or words that I want to keep on the same line no matter what.

Non-breaking Hyphens work the same way, but the hyphenated word won't split in the middle. This is the perfect solution for people with hyphenated names.

109. Adding a Non-Breaking Space

Instead of pressing the spacebar, **use the keyboard shortcut CTRL-SHIFT-SPACEBAR**.

When **SHOW/HIDE ¶** is on, there's a tiny circle instead of a dot between the words.

When one of the words with non-breaking spaces reaches the end of the row, the entire phrase wraps to the next line.

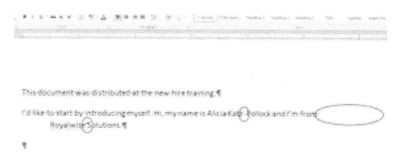

110. Adding a Non-Breaking Hyphen

Instead of typing a normal dash, **use the keyboard shortcut CTRL-SHIFT-HYPHEN (DASH).**

There's no difference in the character that appears, but if the second word reaches the end of the line, both words now wrap to the next row.

Drop Caps

Drop Caps harken back to the days of old-fashioned printed books. Remember those big fancy letters at the beginning of a chapter that added panache to printed text?

A Drop Cap spans several rows of text, indenting the paragraph around it, or can be placed in the margin.

111. Inserting a Drop Cap

Click in the first paragraph of the content. It doesn't matter if I select the first character or not.

Go to the INSERT ribbon and click on DROP CAP.

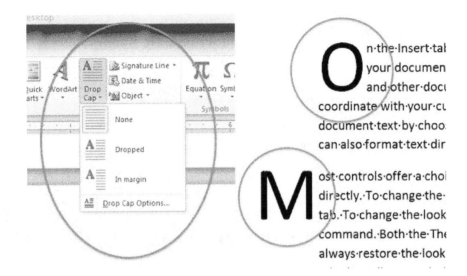

Choose either DROPPED or IN MARGIN.

The first letter of the paragraph instantly becomes a Drop Cap.

112. Setting Drop Cap Options

To adjust the appearance of the Drop Cap, **click DROP CAP OPTIONS on the ribbon button**.

In the dialog box, **switch the Drop Cap style, pick a different font, change the number of rows the character takes up, or move the character closer to or farther from the text**.

Hyperlinks

When I type an email address or website URL in a document, Word automatically turns the text into a clickable hyperlink. That's great for viewing on a computer, but not practical for printed documents. Here's how to manage hyperlinks, and remove the formatting when the underlining isn't wanted.

113. Automatic Hyperlinks

Type an email address, or a URL that starts with www or http, and press the SPACEBAR or ENTER. The address becomes an active hyperlink, colored blue and underlined.

Hold the CTRL key down and click the link to open an email message or web browser with that address.

http://www.royalwise.com
Ctrl+Click to follow link

http://www.royalwise.com

114. Removing Hyperlinks

If the document is to be printed, and not viewed onscreen, this formatting should be removed.

Hold the cursor over the TINY BLUE-AND-WHITE RECTANGLE at the beginning of the link, and it pops up an AUTOCORRECT SMARTTAG. Click it, and choose either UNDO HYPERLINK, or STOP AUTOMATICALLY CREATING HYPERLINKS to stop all hyperlinks in this document.

Alternatively, right-click on the hyperlink and choose REMOVE HYPERLINK.

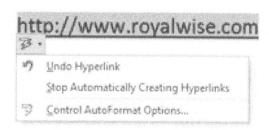

To permanently stop this behavior from happening, **go to FILE→OPTIONS→ PROOFING and Click on the AUTOCORRECT OPTIONS button. On** *both* **the**

AUTOFORMAT and AUTOFORMAT AS YOU TYPE tabs, turn off the checkmarks for INTERNET AND NETWORK PATHS WITH HYPERLINKS.

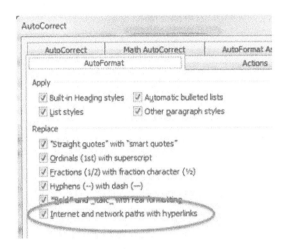

115. Hyperlinks to Documents and Targets

Hyperlinks can be more than just Internet addresses.

Hyperlinks can also open documents, create blank documents, and jump to different parts of a file.

On the INSERT ribbon, click on HYPERLINK. Alternatively, right-click on an existing link and choose EDIT HYPERLINK.

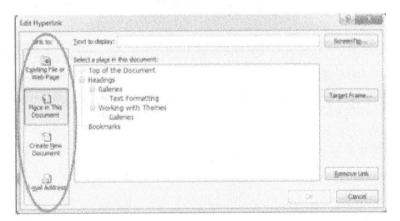

EXISTING FILE OR WEBPAGE

- In **TEXT TO DISPLAY, type the text** that will show in the document.
- If it's a **WEBPAGE, type the URL in the ADDRESS: BOX** at the bottom.
- If it's a **FILE, navigate to the file** on the computer. **The target file MUST also be included** to send this document to other people!

Notice that there are shortcuts to recent webpages and files.

PLACE IN THIS DOCUMENT

Heading Styles and Bookmarks can be used as targets. **In TEXT TO DISPLAY, I can type what I want the link to say. Pick the destination off the list**.

CREATE NEW DOCUMENT

Use this option to generate a new document on the fly.

OpenType Font Formatting

OpenType fonts are specially designed for professional layout. Certain fonts, including the Microsoft ClearType Collection (Calibri, Cambria, Candara, Consolas, Constantia, and Corbel) contain OpenType features including small caps, ligatures, number forms, and number spacing. Gabriola, a Windows 7 font, is particularly feature-rich.

Instead of each letter being individually drawn, specific letter combinations are designed together as one glyph.

For example, after I type "fi" or "ffi," OpenType fonts replace the characters with one glyph created by the font designer. This aids in legibility.

Ligatures: Candara:
NONE: five spiffy flowers.
STANDARD: five spiffy flowers.

116. Ligatures

If I'm using an OpenType font, I **launch the FONT dialog box from the HOME ribbon, or press CTRL-D**.

Click on the ADVANCED Tab to refine that font's behavior.

- **STANDARD** are the ligatures typographers generally turn into glyphs.
- **STANDARD AND CONTEXTUAL** may include additional ligatures created by the font designer.
- **HISTORICAL AND DISCRETIONARY** may include ligatures that have fallen out of current usage.

117. Number Spacing and Number Forms

The default **NUMBER SPACING** is defined by the font designer.

- **PROPORTIONAL** spaced numbers have variable widths: a 4 is wider than a 1. Candara, Constantia, and Corbel are set to Proportional by default.
- **TABULAR** spaced numbers all have the same width, and line up well underneath each other. Cambria, Calibri, and Consolas are set to Tabular by default.

The default **NUMBER FORM** is also set by the designer.

- **LINING** numbers all have the same height and don't extend below the baseline. Cambria, Calibri, and Consolas are set to Lining by default.
- **OLD-STYLE** numbers may be higher than text characters, or extend below the baseline. Candara, Constantia, and Corbel are set to Old-Style by default.

Number Spacing and Forms:

Lining Tabular	Old-style Tabular
$123,456,789.00	$123,456,789.00
Lining Proportional	Old-style Proportional
$123,456,789.00	$123,456,789.00

118. Stylistic Sets

Stylistic sets add frills and flair to OpenType text. The larger the number, the more the adornment. In Gabriola, Stylistic Set 7 adds old-fashioned calligraphy to the content.

Fonts that I didn't think had any jazz to them really surprised me!

If the top or bottom scrolling gets cut off, adjust its **Paragraph Spacing.**

Stylistic sets:	Gabriola:
Default:	OpenType sure makes flowery letters!
Style Set 3:	OpenType sure makes flowery letters!
Style Set 5:	OpenType sure makes flowery letters!
Style Set 7:	OpenType sure makes flowery letters!

119. Use Contextual Alternates

If the font designer was so inclined, the letters may change shape depending on the text around them.

This is d

This is di

This is different.

Replicating Text Formatting

Once I've formatted my text, I may want to use that appearance later. I don't need to go to each instance of text and apply the same font, size, color, and effects over and over.

I can replicate the font formatting in a number of ways.

120. Save As a Style

Styles are one of the most powerful tools in Word.

Styles allow me to apply a set of character and paragraph formatting to text in one step. They also allow me to modify one instance of that style and have the change cascade down throughout the document to the rest.

To save formatted text as a Style, **right-click on it, highlight STYLE, and choose SAVE SELECTION AS A NEW QUICK STYLE. Give the Style a name.** My new Style now appears in the Styles gallery on the Home Tab.

Select the next text and click the button in the GALLERY to instantly apply all the same formats.

To change the Style, **make the modification to the text, right-click on the STYLE in the gallery, and choose UPDATE [NAME] TO MATCH SELECTION.** All the samples of that Style in the document instantly take on the modification.

that you specify directly. To change the overall look of your document, choose new Theme elements on the Page Layout tab. To change the looks available in the Quick Style gallery, use the Change Current Quick Style Set command. Both the Themes gallery and the Quick Styles gallery provide reset commands so that you can always restore the look of your document to the original

121. The Format Painter

The Format Painter applies an entire collection of custom formats with just one click.

Click in the text that has the desired format (this is the hardest step to remember). **On the HOME ribbon, click on the FORMAT PAINTER button on the left side in the CLIPBOARD group.** Notice that the cursor now has a paintbrush attached to it.

Drag across the next text. It instantly takes on all the formatting from the first.

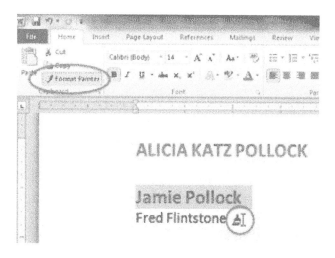

If there are several places that need that formatting, don't perform each formatting duplication individually. The Format Painter can apply the settings to several items, much like a painter dipping her brush into a color and then dabbing the canvas repeatedly.

Click on the formatted text; this time, instead of clicking one time on the FORMAT PAINTER button, click on it TWICE. The cursor has the same brush, but it also now has a + on it. Drag across as many locations as needed.

Be careful when in Format Painter mode—the special effects apply to any object clicked on.

When done duplicating the formatting, either **click on the FORMAT PAINTER button again to turn it off**, or simply **press the ESC key** in the upper left corner of the keyboard.

122. Apply to Multiple Selections

To select text in several locations at once, **hold down the CTRL key when dragging across** each occurrence.

When applying a format using any button on the ribbon, it's applied to all of the selections at the same time, with just one click!

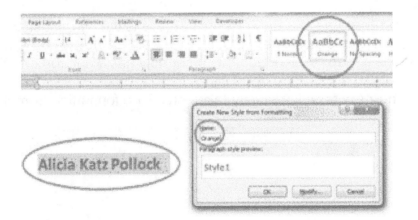

123. Use Keyboard Shortcuts

Click in text that has the formatting to replicate, and press CTRL-SHIFT-C. It'll copy the formatting, but not the text itself.

Highlight the target text and press CTRL-SHIFT-V to paste the formatting.

This last tip will make you a reformatting superstar!

Clear Formatting

It's really frustrating when I press Enter, and the next line carries forward my formatting, even if I don't want it to.

124. The Clear Formatting Button

Instead of turning off every single format setting, **select the text, then use the CLEAR FORMATTING button on the HOME ribbon**.

One click brings the text back to the Normal style.

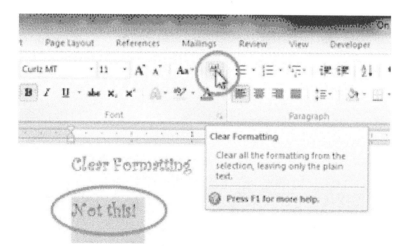

125. Ctrl-Spacebar

I can also clear the formatting using a keyboard command.

Select the text and press CTRL-SPACEBAR.

CHAPTER 8: PARAGRAPH FORMATTING

"Paragraph Formatting" refers to the position of the text on the page, from justification to line spacing. These Tips raise your understanding of proper word processing techniques.

Paragraph Spacing

Word defines a "paragraph" as every time I press Enter, or in other words, everything between two ¶ marks. A paragraph can be a blank line, a heading, or a giant block of text.

By default, Word inserts a blank space between my paragraphs. This is because most people have a bad habit of pressing Enter an extra time to create a blank line. Not only are those extra keystrokes, but if you've ever tried to squeeze content onto one page by shrinking all those spaces, you made yourself a lot of extra work.

126. Normal vs. No Spacing

By default, Word inserts 10 points of space between paragraphs. That's slightly smaller than one blank line.

If I don't want that gap at all, **I select the whole document (CTRL-A) and click NO SPACING in the STYLES GALLERY on the HOME ribbon.**

127. Paragraph Spacing Before and After

To adjust how much space appears between paragraphs, **select the text, then go to the PAGE LAYOUT ribbon.**

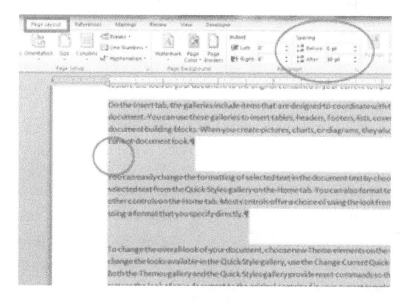

In the PARAGRAPH GROUP are stepper arrows, which widen or narrow the space in 6pt increments.

BEFORE adjusts the space above the paragraph. This is great for creating a gap between sections of a document.

AFTER adjusts the space below the paragraph. This creates whitespace to help the document's readability.

Click on the LAUNCHER BUTTON in the corner of the PARAGRAPH group to view these same settings in the Paragraph dialog box.

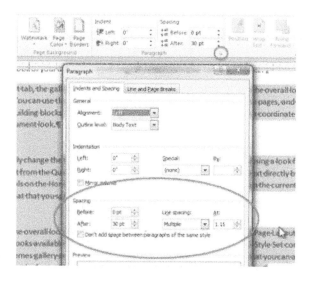

Another place to add or remove Paragraph Spacing is on the HOME Tab.

Click on the Line Spacing button, and look at the bottom two options. If the paragraph already has spacing, they say **REMOVE SPACE BEFORE/AFTER**. If there is no spacing, they read **ADD SPACE BEFORE/AFTER**. Using this adds 10pts of space.

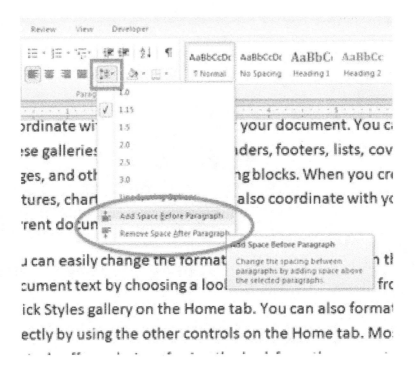

128. Soft Returns

To create a line break, which splits text onto two lines and still has them act as one paragraph (i.e., no space between them), **do a SHIFT-ENTER.** This puts a **SOFT RETURN** between the lines.

This is frequently used on flyers when one idea needs two lines for spacing and emphasis.

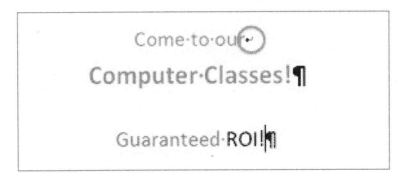

129. Changing the Default Paragraph Style

If the automatic 10pt spacing between paragraphs is annoying, just turn it off.

Go to FILE→OPTIONS→ADVANCED→EDITING OPTIONS, find DEFAULT PARAGRAPH STYLE and change the drop-down to NO SPACING.

I do recommend getting used to the automatic spacing before turning it off. If you've been using Word for a decade, you've become desensitized to one of your bad habits!

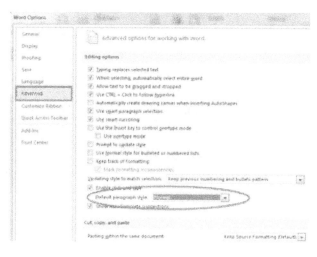

First Line Indents

When I write an essay, I indent the first line of every paragraph so that the reader knows where each idea begins. In business, the convention is to instead **leave a space between paragraphs**.

What I NEVER do is press the Spacebar five times! Word has several tools to manage First Line Indents.

130. The Tab Key

Most people habitually indent a paragraph by pressing the Tab key on the keyboard. This jumps the cursor to the right 1/2 inch.

Turn on the SHOW/HIDE ¶ button on the HOME ribbon to see the → mark for each tab.

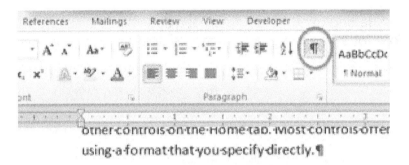

131. Paragraph→Special→First Line

The drawback to using Tabs is that I'm inserting an extra keystroke every time, and leaving myself open to inconsistent formatting. Instead, I let Word automatically indent every new paragraph for me.

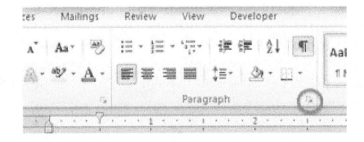

Select all paragraphs that need an indent (new ones adopt this setting automatically). **Click on the LAUNCHER BUTTON in the PARAGRAPH group on the HOME ribbon. In the Paragraph dialog box, change SPECIAL: to FIRST LINE**.

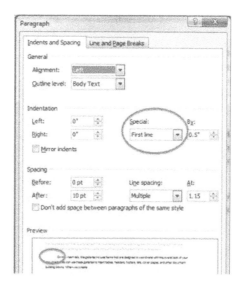

132. Using the Ruler

See our chapter on **using the Ruler to Set First Line Indents**.

133. Troubleshooting

Sometimes when I press Tab, Word formats the Tab as a First Line indent instead. I can tell because when I have Show/Hide ¶ on, there's no Tab arrow, and I can see the First Line indent mark on the Ruler.

When Word autoformats this way, I also see a yellow Smart Tag. It gives me the option of **CHANGE BACK TO TAB (this one time), or STOP SETTING INDENT ON TABS AND BACKSPACE**. The latter prevents First Line Indents permanently.

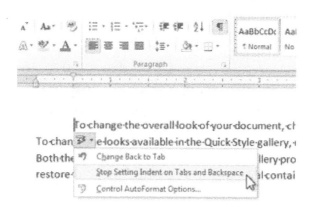

Also, **watch out for CENTERED text**. Check if the ruler shows a First Line Indent. If it does, the text is NOT really centered! **Move the FIRST LINE INDENT RULER ARROW back to the margin,** and centered text properly aligns.

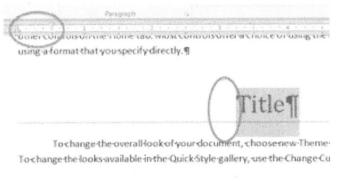

Working With Tabs

When I look at the Ruler, I see slightly larger marks at the inch and half-inch measurements. And when I press Tab on my keyboard, my cursor jumps along those 1/2-inch increments.

I like to set custom Tabs to my own measurements, allowing me to line up content without using columns or tables. There's a dialog box for this buried deep within the **PARAGRAPH FORMATTING window under the TABS button**, but it's much easier to set the Tab Stops right on the ruler.

134. Adding Left, Center, Right, Decimal, and Bar Tabs

To the left of the Ruler is a box with what looks like an L in it, but it's actually a Left Tab Stop. **Click this box repeatedly to toggle through the LEFT, CENTER, RIGHT, DECIMAL, AND BAR TABS, plus the FIRST LINE INDENT AND HANGING INDENT MARKERS**.

LEFT, CENTER, AND RIGHT are self-explanatory. **DECIMAL TABS** line up all numbers on their decimal points. The **BAR TAB** draws a vertical line down the page — it's great for dividing tabbed content into columns.

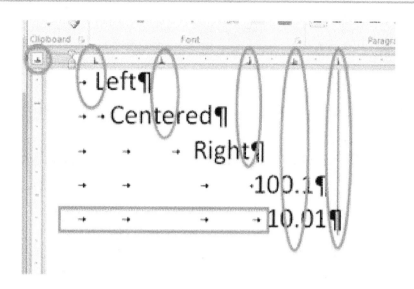

To use ruler Tabs, **pick the TAB STYLE, then click on the RULER to create the TAB STOP** (all the half-inch default Tabs to the left of this custom Tab disappear). **Press the TAB KEY on the keyboard** to jump to the new Tab setting.

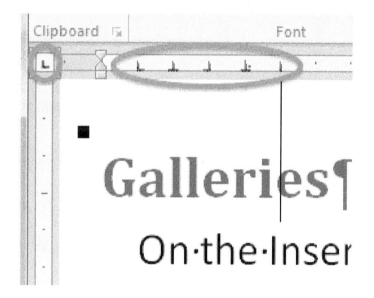

135. Moving Tabs

If the new Tab didn't land in exactly the right place, or it needs some fine-tuning, **click on the TAB MARK on the RULER and drag it left or right** to adjust the position. The text moves with it.

136. Adding Tab Leaders

Tab Leaders are the ....marks between content and page numbers in a Table of Contents or phone list. Never type these manually using periods or underlines! By using Tab Leaders, the number of dots adjusts automatically with the length of the content.

Double-click on a TAB to open the Tab Settings box to manually type in new Tab Stops, and set Leaders.

To add a Dot Leader, **click on the desired TAB MEASUREMENT in the list, change LEFT/CENTER/RIGHT if needed, click on the LEADER STYLE, and be sure to click the SET button.**

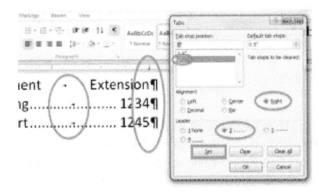

137. Deleting Tabs

If a Tab is no longer needed, **click on it and DRAG IT DOWN off the RULER.** The content jumps forward to the next available Tab, until a new Tab is added nearby.

Line and Paragraph Breaks

At the end of a page, Word wraps the content to the next page automatically. While most of the time that's great news, sometimes I need to keep particular content together.

To work with these options, **select the desired content, and use the LAUNCHER BUTTON in the HOME ribbon to view the PARAGRAPH DIALOG BOX. Click on the LINE AND PAGE BREAKS TAB.**

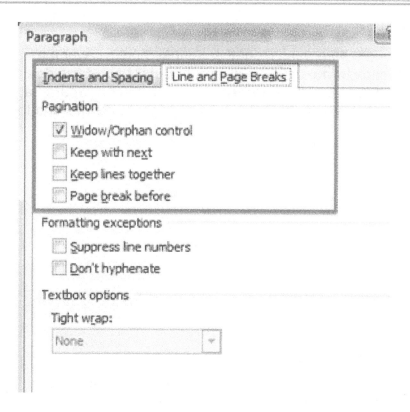

138. Widow/Orphan Control

By default, Word never leaves just the first line of a paragraph at the bottom of a page (a "widow"), or just the last line at the top of a page (an "orphan"). Instead, it splits the paragraph in the middle, or moves the entire thing to the text page. This may leave a gap at the bottom of a page, especially if there's a footnote there.

Click on the checkmark to turn off WIDOW/ORPHAN CONTROL, and the text flows to the bottom of the page no matter what.

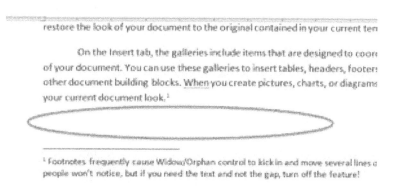

139. Keep With Next

To keep two or more paragraphs together so that there's never a page break between them, **click in the top paragraph, or select all of the desired paragraphs, and turn on KEEP WITH NEXT**. If the second paragraph moves to the next page, the first one goes too. This works well for headlines and table rows.

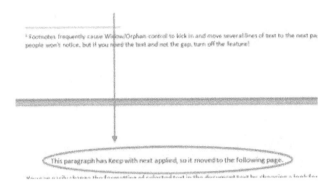

140. Keep Lines Together

This works the same as Keep With Next, but refers to lines instead of full paragraphs. This way I can prevent particular rows from breaking across two pages, even if they're in the same paragraph.

Select the rows to be joined, go into the PARAGRAPH DIALOG BOX, and select KEEP LINES TOGETHER.

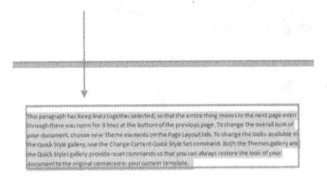

141. Page Break Before

Adding **PAGE BREAK BEFORE** to text attaches a Page Break to the content itself, instead of adding it in manually.

This is great when rearranging my document, so I don't have to modify the pagination every time. The page break moves with the text.

Here's one of my favorite Hot Tips: I frequently modify **Heading styles** to include this formatting.

For example, I add it to Heading 1 and Heading 2 so that they always start on a new page, without my having to insert a Next Page Break every single time.

CHAPTER 9: PAGE LAYOUT

"Page Layout" refers to how text flows on the page, from margins to columns to where the next page begins.

These Tips & Tricks help control the appearance of every page.

Page Breaks

When I want to skip the blank space at the end of a page and force the content to start again on the next one, I don't press Enter repeatedly until it moves there. If I did, I'd create a series of paragraph breaks, and if I later change my font size, margins, line spacing, or rearrange the document, I'd then have to delete (or add more of) these paragraph marks.

Instead, I insert a Manual Page Break to force the rest of the content to start at the top of the following page.

142. Insert→Page Break

Place the cursor at the beginning of the text to be forced to the next page. Click on the INSERT ribbon and then on the PAGE BREAK button.

Turn on the SHOW/HIDE ¶ button to see a dotted Page Break line at the end of the content on the previous page.

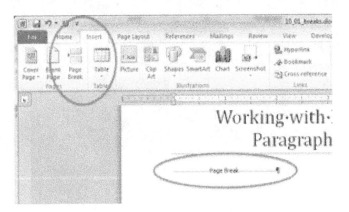

143. Page Layout→Break

Place the cursor at the beginning of the text to be forced to the next page. **Click on the PAGE LAYOUT ribbon, then on the BREAKS button.** The top option, **PAGE**, gives the same result as other Page Break button. We'll explore some of these other options in future chapters.

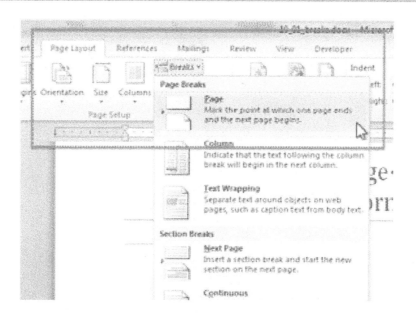

144. CTRL-Enter

To enter a Page Break while typing, without taking my hands off they keyboard, I **press the keyboard shortcut CTRL-ENTER**.

The cursor jumps to the next page, and I don't even have to stop typing.

Section Breaks

Section breaks allow me to change page and paragraph formatting in a way that my settings don't have to apply to the whole document. Section Breaks can start a new page, or just mark locations where there are changes to the layout.

Examples of Section Breaks include: restarting the numbering to have a preface with roman numerals, making a single page landscape orientation instead of portrait, or creating **columns**.

145. Next Page Section Breaks

Place the cursor at the beginning of the text to be forced to the next page. **Click PAGE LAYOUT→BREAKS→NEXT PAGE.**

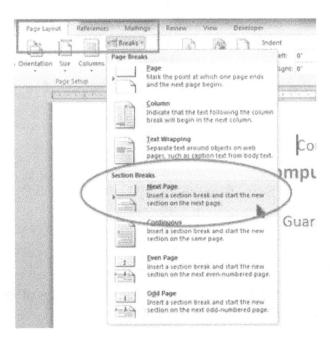

Turn on the SHOW/HIDE ¶ button to see double dotted lines at the end of the content on the upper page.

When applying any type of paragraph or page layout formatting, look for a setting at the bottom of the dialog box that says APPLY TO:. **Be sure APPLY TO: says SECTION instead of WHOLE DOCUMENT**.

146. Continuous Section Breaks

This allows different formatting above and below the line, but on the same page. **Columns**, for example, use Continuous Section Breaks. The procedure is exactly the same as above, but **choose PAGE LAYOUT→ BREAKS→CONTINUOUS from the drop-down lis**t.

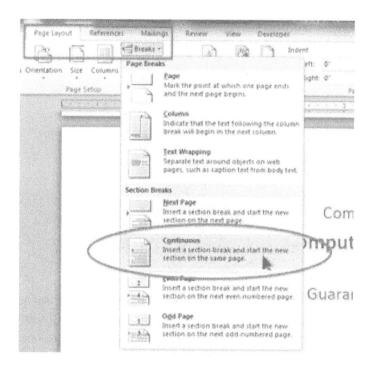

147. Even and Odd Section Breaks

In books, chapters usually begin on the right, odd-numbered pages. Don't spend any time adding extra page breaks to force this to happen, especially since later edits may break this alignment.

Even and Odd Section Breaks not only force the content to the top of a new page, like a Next Page Section Break, they also ensure that the content always starts on the left or right side of facing pages.

In other words, when I insert an Odd Page Section Break at the beginning of a book chapter, the chapter always starts on the odd, right side page.

To create these page breaks, **choose PAGE LAYOUT→ BREAKS→EVEN PAGE or ODD PAGE from the drop-down list.**

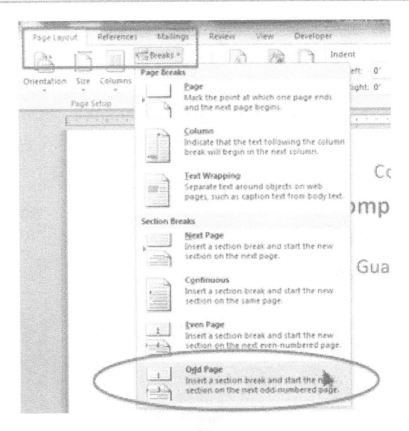

If needed, Word automatically inserts a blank page for the left-hand evenly numbered page. This extra page may not show in Print Layout view, but it's not an error. I can see all the pages while in Print Preview. Be sure to keep an eye out for this: the page numbering skips the even numbers.

Columns

Before Word 2010, laying out page content in columns required inserting section breaks before and after the content...and jumping through a few hoops.

Now, it couldn't be easier.

Here are a few Tips & Tricks to customize your columns even further.

148. Formatting Columns

To lay out my content in columns, I **select it, then go to the PAGE LAYOUT ribbon and click on COLUMNS**.

Choose the number of columns. There are also options for a narrow left or right sidebar.

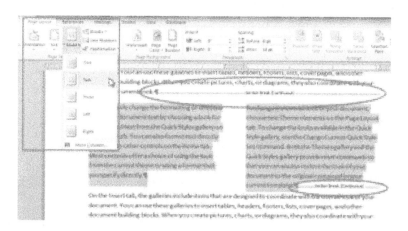

My text instantly aligns itself in columns. **Click on the SHOW/HIDE ¶ button to see the Section Breaks Word inserted**.

If the first paragraph after my columns is too close, I **insert extra PARAGRAPH SPACING ABOVE.**

Choosing 1 COLUMN returns my column-formatted text straight across the page again, as it is normally.

149. More Columns

Those default 1, 2 or 3 column layouts are great, but I can also take complete control over the dimensions.

At the bottom of the Columns button, **click on MORE COLUMNS**.

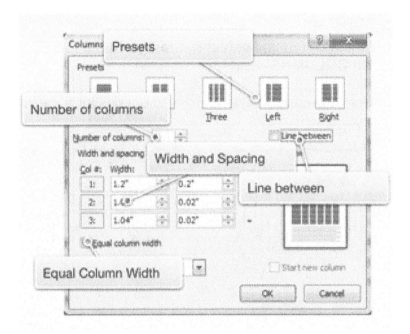

The top 5 buttons are the same presets from the ribbon button's drop-down.

Below that, I can **type in the number of columns I want**, up to 13.

The next section, Width and Spacing, allows me to manually **specify how wide each column is, and the size of the gap between them.** When I change one dimension, the rest update accordingly.

Below the 3 column width boxes, there's a checkmark for **EQUAL COLUMN WIDTH. Uncheck this box to create columns of any width and spacing**.

Note that when adjusting a column or its spacing, the other dimensions also adjust — this way the columns won't be wider than the margins.

On the right side of the window is a checkmark for **LINE BETWEEN. This places a vertical line between all the columns, making a great sidebar.**

At the bottom is a drop-down to **apply these columns settings either to the TEXT SELECTED before entering this dialog box, the ENTIRE SECTION, or the ENTIRE DOCUMENT**.

150. Column Breaks

To force content to start at the top of the next column, I **click the cursor where I want to begin, then click PAGE LAYOUT→BREAKS→COLUMN**.

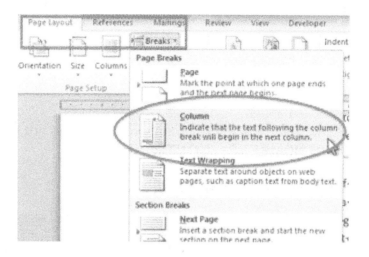

151. Balancing Columns

If one of the columns comes out very long while the other is very short, balance them to equal length.

Click at the end of the last column, before the section break, and click PAGE LAYOUT→BREAKS→CONTINUOUS.

All the columns are now within one line of each other in length.

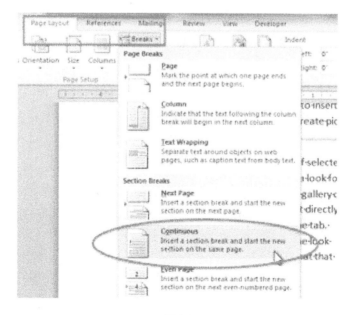

Line Numbering

Law offices, research facilities, and collaborators frequently reference a specific line in a document by number. There's no need to type these in manually, or use Numbering to create them.

Word has a powerful and flexible line numbering tool.

152. Applying Line Numbers

To apply line numbering to the entire document, content need not be selected. **Click PAGE LAYOUT→LINE NUMBERS→CONTINUOUS.**

Numbers appear in the left margin of the entire document.

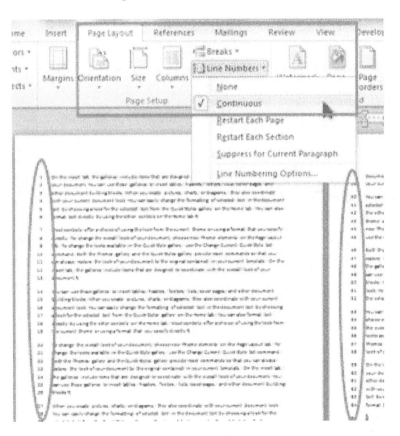

153. Restarting Line Numbers

To start each page over again at 1, on the same **LINE NUMBERS drop-down**, choose **RESTART EACH PAGE**.

To start the numbering over again anywhere on a page, **insert a CONTINUOUS SECTION BREAK and select RESTART EACH SECTION**.

154. Suppressing Line Numbers

To skip a paragraph's numbering, **click in it, then choose PAGE LAYOUT→ SUPPRESS FOR CURRENT PARAGRAPH**.

155. Advanced Options

Take even greater control by **choosing LINE NUMBERING OPTIONS at the bottom of the drop-down, then on the LINE NUMBERS... button at the bottom of the dialog box**.

From this window I can **start with numbers other than 1, change the distance of the numbers from the text, and increment the count by more than one**.

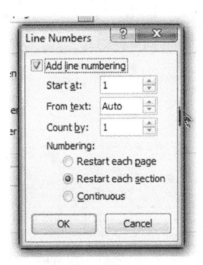

Vertically Centering a Cover Page

Cover pages traditionally locate the title about ⅓ to halfway down the page.

Don't press Enter repeatedly to get there!

Instead, follow these steps to center the page vertically, from top to bottom.

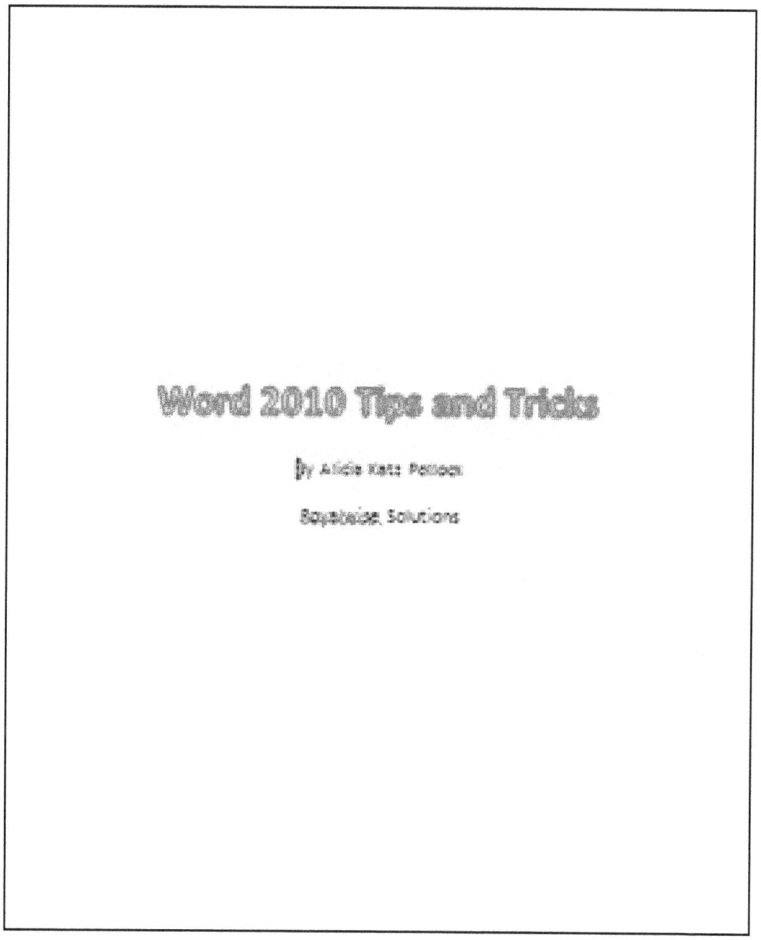

Word 2010 Tips and Tricks

by Alicia Katz Pollock

Bayalside Solutions

156. Insert a Next Page Section Break

Click the cursor at the beginning of the text to appear on page 2. Go to the Page Layout→Breaks and click on NEXT PAGE in the SECTION BREAKS area.

Click back on the cover page.

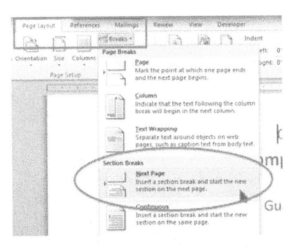

157. Center the Page Vertically

Go to the PAGE LAYOUT ribbon and click on the LAUNCHER BUTTON in the bottom right corner of the PAGE SETUP GROUP.

Change VERTICAL ALIGNMENT: to either Center or Justified.

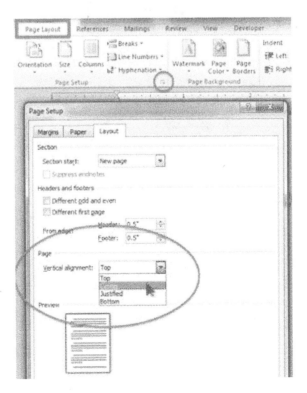

Center drops the text to the middle of the page from top to bottom, as shown in the first image.

Justified spreads out the lines so that they are evenly spaced.

Word 2010 Tips and Tricks

By Allison Kaye Pelland

Realwide Solutions

CHAPTER 10: STYLES

Using Styles to format your text is more powerful and efficient than applying several levels of formatting.

Styles

When applying the same character and paragraph formatting several times throughout a document, save dozens of repetitive steps by applying a Style instead. Word comes with dozens of pre-designed Style sets, and I can modify them or create new ones at any time.

An added bonus of using the Heading 1 and Heading 2 styles is that Word looks for them when building a Table of Contents, cross-referencing, **exporting to PowerPoint**, labeling **Figures and Captions**, and for several other techniques.

158. Apply a Style

Select the text to stylize, then **go to the HOME ribbon**. On the right is a Style Gallery—**click on the MORE DROP-DOWN button to see a list of character styles**. This isn't all of the styles available, but it's a great start.

Pick the style, and the text changes accordingly. For example, choosing Heading 1 makes my text 14pt, bold, blue, with **24pt Space Before**, **Keep With Next**, and **Keep Lines Together**. All that in one click!

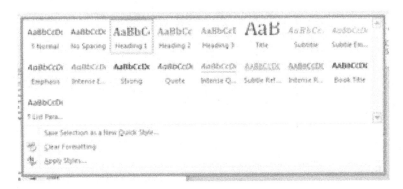

159. Modify an Existing Style

Once I've applied a Style throughout a document, modifying that Style updates all instances of it at the same time.

For example, if I change Heading 1 to centered and **Page Break Before**, all my Heading 1's instantly jump to the top of a new page and become center aligned.

To trigger this cascading effect, **make the changes to the text, then right-click on the STYLE in the Gallery. Choose UPDATE [STYLE] TO MATCH SELECTION**.

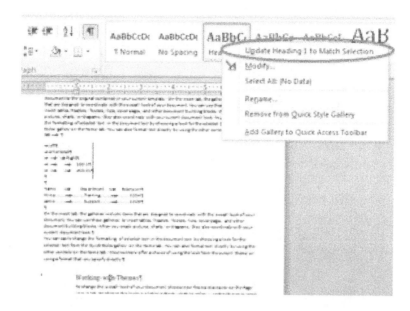

Alternatively, **click on MODIFY...** to go into a dialog box and make all the formatting changes there.

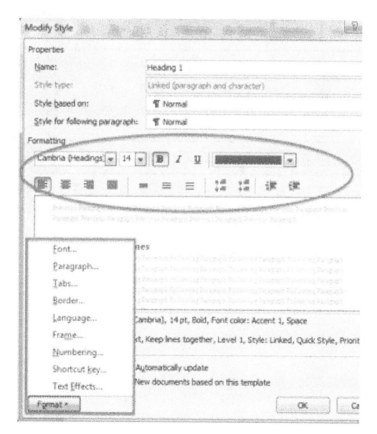

The **FORMAT button** in the bottom left corner allows me to modify the Font, Paragraph, Tabs, Borders, Numbering, Text Effects, and more.

160. Create a New Style

If I apply a series of character and paragraph formatting to text, and plan to use that appearance again, I turn it into a new Style so that I can apply all the settings instantly in just one click.

Select the formatted text, right-click on it, choose STYLES off the shortcut menu, and then click SAVE SELECTION AS A NEW QUICK STYLE.

Give it a name, and **the new Style appears in the Gallery** for future use.

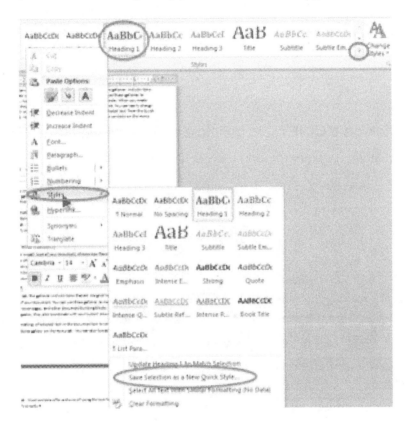

Advanced Style Settings

Once you're comfortable with applying Styles, modifying them, and creating new ones, here are a few more tricks you may like.

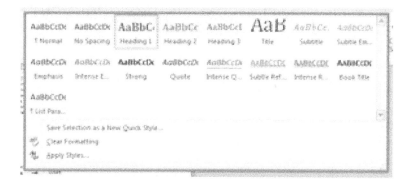

161. Basing New Styles on Existing Styles

After I've worked hard to design a Style, but then need a variation, I don't need to start from scratch. This technique also cascades updates — if I change the original, the new one also absorbs the new formatting.

For example, let's say I've **created a new Style** called Heading Plus, that started as a Heading 1 but I added a **bottom hairline border** and centering. If I turn Heading 1 from blue to green, Heading Plus also turns green.

To do this, **start by applying the original Style, then make the formatting changes. Save the text as a new style**. Now, **right-click on the new Style in the gallery, and choose MODIFY...**

If **STYLE BASED ON:** has the name of the original Style, it cascades as described. **If it says "NORMAL," change it to the desired base style.**

162. Saving Styles for Future Use

By default, changes to my Style gallery only are valid for the current document. To make them available to all Word documents, **go into the MODIFY STYLE dialog box and move the radio button from ONLY IN THIS DOCUMENT to NEW DOCUMENTS BASED ON THIS TEMPLATE**.

If I'm working in a standard .docx file, all new documents based on the Normal template will show these Style modifications.

If I **save this document as a .DOTX TEMPLATE**, the Styles become available in all new documents based on this Template.

163. Automatically Updating Styles

When I modify my Styles constantly and don't want to have to **update them manually each time**, I set the Style to cascade as soon as I change its formatting in the document. **Check off AUTOMATICALLY UPDATE at the bottom of the MODIFY STYLE dialog box.**

However, BE VERY CAREFUL when using this setting. I can't alter one instance of a Style without all of them changing too. Worse, if I have Styles based on other Styles, changes to a root Style affects all other related Styles in the document.

This can have severe, confusing consequences! If while working on a document I change the formatting in one location, and several other headings change, here's a good troubleshooting tip: Figure out which is the root Style and uncheck Automatically Update. Then, do the same for all subsequent cascading styles.

Keyboard Shortcuts for Styles

If I apply the same Styles over and over, it's faster to use a keyboard shortcut than to visit the Styles gallery every time. Utilizing this technique will prove to any employer that you *KNOW* Word, and you're worth your weight in keyboards!

164. Assign a Keyboard Shortcut

To assign a keyboard shortcut to a Style, **right-click on the Style in the Gallery,**

and choose MODIFY....

In the Modify Styles dialog box, **click the FORMAT button in the bottom left corner, and choose SHORTCUT KEY**.

Type a key combination that's easy to remember. See if it's already been assigned to anything. If it has, don't override the previous keystroke unless it's something completely obscure.

I can **save the changes in the NORMAL TEMPLATE** so it works in every Word document, or **drop down the arrow and select the name of just this document**.

CHAPTER 11: TABLES

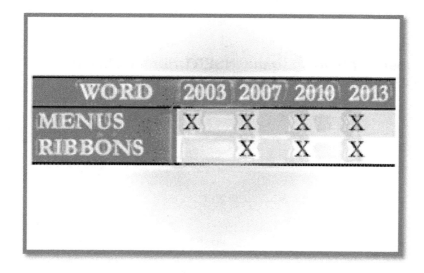

WORD	2003	2007	2010	2013
MENUS	X	X	X	X
RIBBONS		X	X	X

Word 2010's Table tools are quite extensive, yet intuitive. Here are several techniques you may not have stumbled across in your exploration.

Inserting Tables

Most people insert Tables by going to the Insert ribbon, clicking on the Table button, and drawing across the boxes for the number of cells they want.

Here are several other techniques for inserting Tables that automate the process.

165. Text to Tables

If there is already text in the document aligned using **Tab Stops**, I can convert that content into a Table instead of inserting a Table and then dragging the entries into the cells.

Select the tabbed content, go to the INSERT ribbon, click on the TABLE button, and choose INSERT TABLE.... Voilà, a Table!

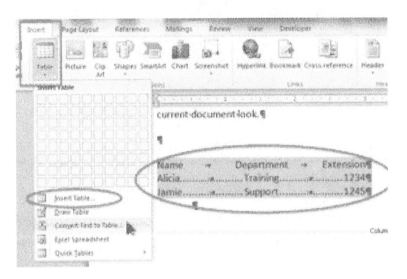

If the content is not tabbed, but instead uses commas or ¶ marks between, **click on CONVERT TEXT TO TABLE** instead. A dialog box asks **how many rows and columns**—usually the default corresponds to the content. **If the list of 12 items would look better as 3 rows and 4 columns, specify those dimensions and the items arrange themselves accordingly.** At the bottom of the dialog box, the delimiter (tabs or commas) is pre-selected.

Note that I can also do the opposite—turn any table into tab, paragraph, or comma-delimited text.

Select the Table, go to the TABLE TOOLS→LAYOUT tab, and click the CONVERT TO TEXT button on the far right.

At the bottom, **choose how to separate the content. Click OK in the dialog box that appears**, and the content aligns.

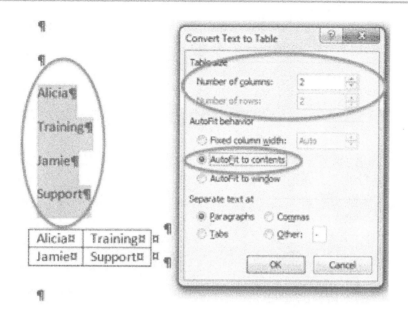

166. AutoFit to Contents

By default, when Word inserts a Table, it reaches across the page from margin to margin. Tables usually look better when the width is adjusted to the length of the content.

Hold the cursor over the vertical lines until it becomes a DOUBLE-HEADED ARROW, then double-click. The cells shrink to fit the longest entry in that column.

Instead of making this fix after the content is in, I can also size the cells to fit right off the bat as I create the Table.

When inserting a Table, use the AUTOFIT TO CONTENTS in the dialog box, and the columns always perfectly fit their longest items.

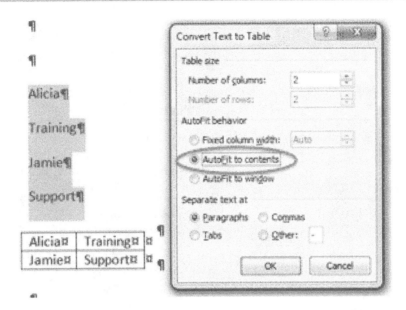

167. Quick Tables

Why start from scratch? **Click on "Quick Tables" at the bottom of the INSERT→ TABLE button** to insert pre-formatted calendars and professionally designed Table layouts.

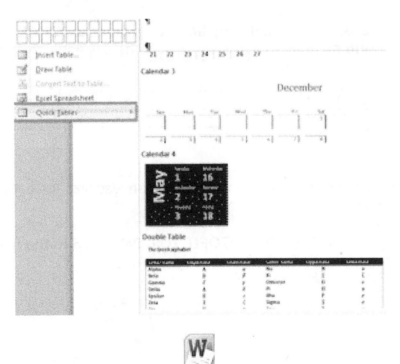

Adding Captions

Long-time Word users remember the days of creating Captions by adding text boxes and grouping them with the Tables and Images.

The process is now automated. Even better, the Captions renumber themselves automatically when rearranging pages or objects.

168. Insert Caption

Captions aren't limited to Tables—they also work for Figures and Images. Because of this flexibility, the button is on the **REFERENCES ribbon. Click on the INSERT CAPTION button.**

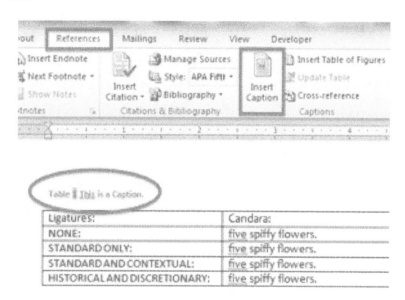

169. Choose a Label

Click on the drop-down arrow next to LABEL and choose TABLE, EQUATION OR FIGURE.

To create a custom Label, **click on the NEW LABEL button**.

To omit the Label with number, and just include the Caption text, **put a checkmark in front of EXCLUDE LABEL FROM CAPTION.**

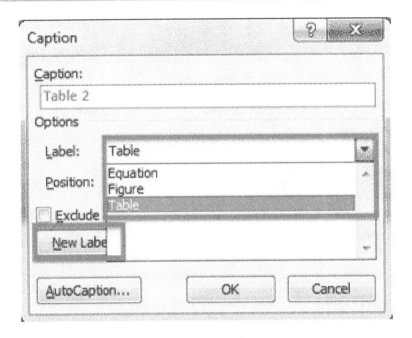

170. Choose a Position

Do I want the Caption above or below the graphic?

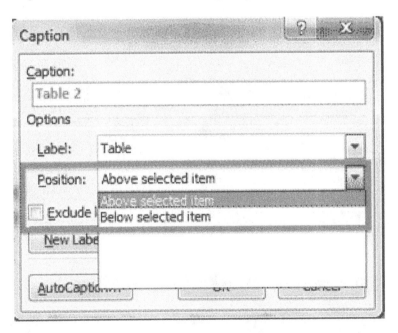

171. Change the Numbering

Click on the NUMBERING... button to change the format of the numbering system. Options include letters and Roman numerals.

I can also **incorporate the chapter number** if properly using **Heading 1, 2, 3 Styles**.

Lastly, there's an option to **change the character used to separate the Label from the Caption name**.

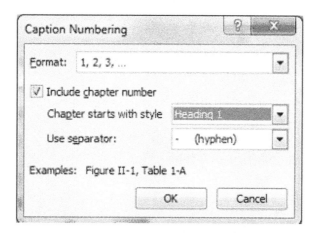

172. AutoCaption New Objects

When inserting multiple Tables, Figures, or Equations, assign Captions automatically instead of repeating these steps for each object.

Click on the AUTOCAPTION button. Place a checkmark in front of all the OBJECT TYPES used in the document. Popular options include "Microsoft Word Table," "Microsoft Excel Worksheet," and "Microsoft PowerPoint Slide."

Click on EACH OPTION, then set the LABEL and POSITION for each OBJECT TYPE. There are also settings for NEW LABEL... and NUMBERING... as described earlier.

Table Tricks

Once you're pretty good with Tables, here are some techniques you want to be sure to know.

173. Tabs Inside a Cell

Pressing the Tab key on my keyboard normally indents text. But in a Table, Tab moves the cursor from cell to cell.

To insert a Tab within a cell, **press Ctrl-TAB.**

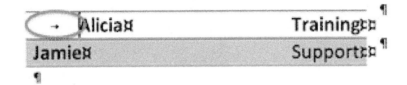

174. Gridlines Only You Can See

Even if I don't want my Table to have any Borders when it prints, it's still helpful to be able to see the Gridlines.

Go to the TABLE TOOLS→LAYOUT ribbon and click on VIEW GRIDLINES.
Faint blue dashes around the cells help visualize the layout.

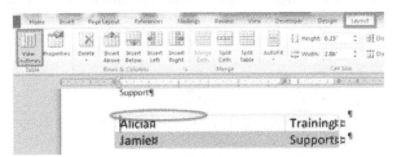

175. Set a Table Style As a Default

If a document always uses one of the Table Styles instead of a plain black-and-white default Table, **right-click on the TABLE STYLE in the Gallery, and select SET AS DEFAULT.**

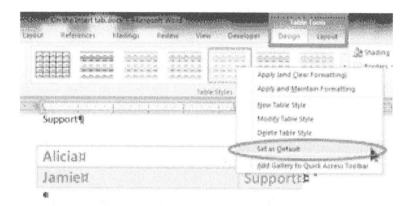

176. Create a Table Style

There are dozens of preset Table Styles on the **TABLE TOOLS→DESIGN ribbon.** Word allows me to create and save my own for future use, exactly like creating **text and paragraph Styles**.

Click on the MORE button in the bottom right corner of the TABLE STYLES Gallery. Choose NEW TABLE STYLE... at the very bottom.

Name the new Table Style.

By default, the table starts plain, but sometimes it's easier to use an existing Table Style as the basis for the new one.

Click on the drop-down for STYLE BASED ON: to specify which pre-formatted Table to use.

Pay special attention to the **APPLY FORMATTING TO:** drop-down. **Choose a PART OF THE TABLE from this list, then set its formatting.** Repeat the procedure for all the necessary Table parts.

Note the Format button in the lower left corner. **Use FORMAT to fine-tune the Table's FONTS, PARAGRAPH SPACING, PROPERTIES, and more**.

This new Table Style is saved only in this document unless I **change the radio button at the bottom to NEW DOCUMENTS BASED ON THIS TEMPLATE. See Advanced Styles for more information** for the ramifications of this option.

CHAPTER 12: GRAPHICS

With Word 2010's new image capabilities, I find myself creating graphics here instead of in "real" graphic programs. Here are essential tools and hidden features to make you feel like a pro.

The Drawing Canvas

The Drawing Canvas is a legacy tool from past versions of Word, before the program juiced up its graphics capabilities. A Drawing Canvas is an object, a bounding box to contain AutoShapes and other content. Use it to provide a background or shading behind shapes and images, or create a wider margin for a text wrap.

177. Turning on the Drawing Canvas

Because the Drawing Canvas is mostly obsolete, it has to be turned on in Word's Options. **Click on FILE→OPTIONS→ADVANCED, and put a check in front of AUTOMATICALLY CREATE DRAWING CANVAS WHEN INSERTING AUTOSHAPES**.

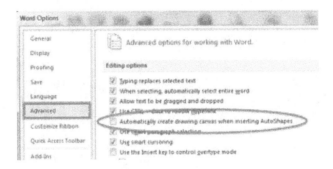

178. Inserting a Drawing Canvas

Go to the INSERT ribbon and click on SHAPES. Click on any shape, and a square appears in the document—this is the Drawing Canvas.

The cursor becomes a crosshair. **Drag inside the DRAWING CANVAS where the shape should go.**

Insert multiple shapes and images inside the Drawing Canvas. If it's moved, all items move together.

179. Formatting the Drawing Canvas

Apply all of Word's FILLS, OUTLINES, AND TEXT WRAP to the Drawing Canvas as if it were any other object.

Moving the Drawing Canvas moves all its contents together.

Taking Screenshots

To include something you see on your screen in your Word document, whether it be info you'd like to discuss, or an error message you want to share, use Word's Screenshot tool to capture it and paste it into your document.

180. Setting Up

The Screenshot tool captures any open window, or just a portion of your choice.

To get ready, set up the graphic on your screen, then go back to Word.

181. Taking a Screenshot of an Entire Window

Place the cursor in the document where the image is to be inserted.

Go to FILE→INSERT ribbon, then click SCREENSHOT.

The dropdown displays thumbnails of all open windows behind Word.

Click on one of the THUMBNAILS, and it will drop into your document at close to full size.

182. Taking a Screenshot of Part of a Window

As before, place the cursor where the image is to be inserted.

Make sure the desired area is visible in the top window.

Go to FILE→INSERT ribbon, then click SCREENSHOT. Click on SCREEN CLIPPING at the bottom of the drop-down.

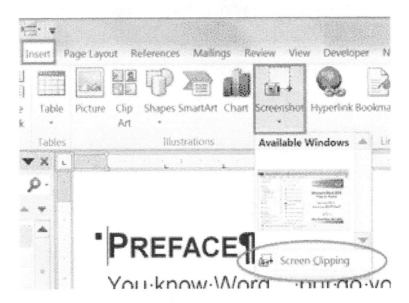

The Word window disappears, and anything behind it is shown in pale gray.

Use the CROSSHAIR to draw a box around the area to capture, starting in the upper left corner and dragging to the lower right. The captured area will display in full color.

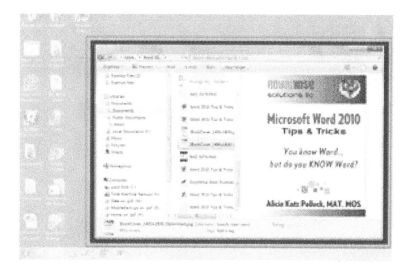

Let go of the mouse button, and the image is instantly placed into the document.

Wrapping Text Around a Graphic

Insert any graphic into a document, and by default Word treats it like a giant alphabet letter. Any text beside it is aligned so that its first line is even with the bottom of the image, with the rest flowing underneath.

Most of the time, it's more effective to float the image on the page so that it can move freely, and the text flows around the graphic.

183. Change the Text Wrap

After inserting any picture, clip art, or graphic into a document, I **click on it to make sure I can see the resize handles around it**. When a graphic is selected, a new **PICTURE TOOLS→FORMAT ribbon** appears at the top of the screen. On the right side of the ribbon, **click on the WRAP TEXT button**.

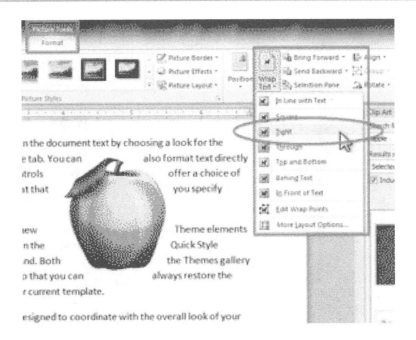

Choose an appropriate Wrap style:

- **IN LINE WITH TEXT** is the default. The graphic acts like a giant alphabet letter. Its size spreads out the lines of text, creating a gap. Moving the image is just like moving text.
- **SQUARE** wraps the text around all four sides of the graphic. This is the most common Wrap style.
- **TIGHT** wraps the text around the shape of clip art and cut out graphics. This looks great for curved images, and graphics with **transparent backgrounds**.
- **THROUGH** allows text to flow into the whitespace of a graphic. To see the full effect, I may need to edit the Wrap points (see below).
- **TOP AND BOTTOM** confines the text to appearing above and below the graphic. The sides remain empty.
- **BEHIND TEXT** layers the text and image so that the image appears in back of the text. Be careful to maintain legibility using font styles & colors.
- **IN FRONT OF TEXT** forces the image to float on top of the content. I won't be able to read the text behind the graphic.

184. Fine-Tune Placement

After setting the Wrap style, drag the image to the desired location. Fine-tune the placement using the ARROWS on the keyboard.

On some keyboards, you may be able to use ALT, CTRL, or other modifier keys to move the image in tinier increments.

Be *very* careful not to orphan words in blank spaces, or interfere with readability.

185. Edit Wrap Points

Editing the Wrap Points helps **control readability and how smoothly the text flows around the graphic**, especially when working with Tight and Through.

To control how close the text is to the image, **click on the image and then on EDIT WRAP POINTS.**

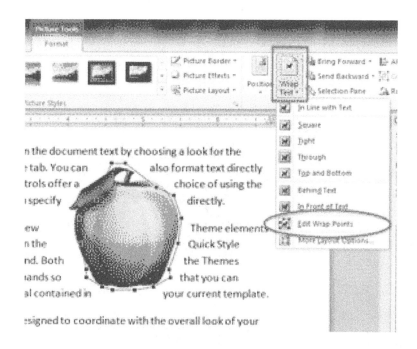

Drag the black dots CLOSER TO and FARTHER FROM the image to adjust the distance to the text. Pulling the dots into an image forces the text closer.

Add ADDITIONAL CONTROL POINTS by clicking on the red line.

186. Default Wrap Styles

Since I almost always need to have my graphics float, I make that the default when I insert new images.

In FILE→OPTIONS→ADVANCED and then in the Cut, Copy, and Paste section, find INSERT/PASTE PICTURES AS: and change IN LINE WITH TEXT to either SQUARE OR TIGHT, whichever is my preference.

Remove Backgrounds and Colors

Word's graphics have certainly come a long way. The new Picture Tools can knock out backgrounds and remove spot color from images.

187. Set Transparent Color

This works best for gifs and drawings with areas of flat color.

After inserting the graphic, click on the COLOR button, then on SET TRANSPARENT COLOR.

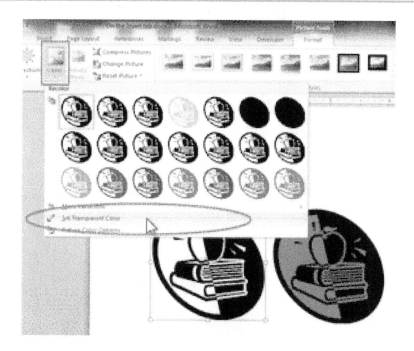

The cursor becomes a pen with a black angle. **Click on the color in the picture to be removed,** and all pixels of that color disappear.

While the removed color looks white, it's actually transparent. If I print on colored paper, the paper color shines through. If I layer this graphic over another, the bottom one peeks through.

188. Remove the Background from an image

This works best with uncluttered backgrounds and edges with contrast, but it's a useful tool nonetheless.

Click on the picture, then on the PICTURE TOOLS→FORMAT Tab. Click on the first button on the ribbon, REMOVE BACKGROUND, and two things happen: the picture sports bright pink coloring, and a new ribbon appears.

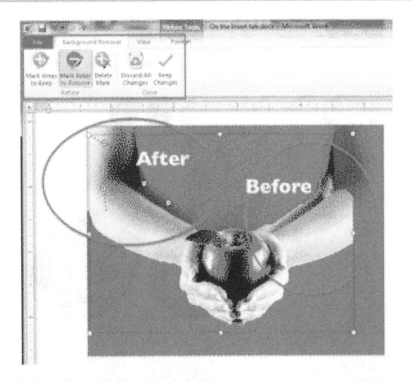

On the ribbon, **MARK AREAS TO KEEP** removes the pink knockout marks from areas I want to save.

Use **MARK AREAS TO REMOVE** to tell Word what to knock out.

Click on either of these buttons and click-and-drag across small segments of the photo to increase or decrease the pink area. Use relatively small lines so that Word can analyze the image to find clear boundaries.

If I make a mistake, I click the DELETE MARK button and click on the + or — sign in the middle of my marks.

When the areas I want to remove are all pink, I click KEEP CHANGES.

If I change my mind and want to cancel, I **click DISCARD ALL CHANGES**.

Editing Clip Art

Sometimes I want to use a Clip Art, but it has the wrong colors, or an element I don't like. It's actually possible to edit graphics found in the Clip Art Gallery. Note that this only works on drawings, not photographs, and not on all of them.

189. Ungroup the Graphic

On the right side of the **PICTURE TOOLS→FORMAT Tab, click on the GROUP button, and then select UNGROUP.**

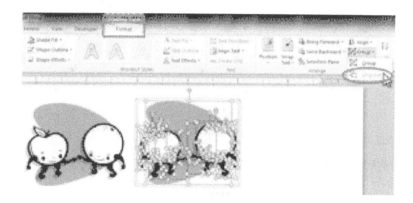

An alert box may appear that says, "This is an imported picture, not a group. Do you want to convert it to a Microsoft Office drawing object?" **Click YES.**

Occasionally, I need to Ungroup twice.

The image changes into a **Drawing Canvas**, with all the elements of the Clip Art broken up into tiny pieces. To see this in action, **click once inside the frame, then press CTRL-A on the keyboard to SELECT ALL.** I now see all the resizing handles for all of the graphic elements. **Click outside the box**—don't change anything yet!

190. Change Colors

Find an element to recolor. **Click on it** (it may take several tries to find the right one if there are a lot of overlapping elements), and **use the DRAWING TOOLS→ SHAPE FILL to change the color**.

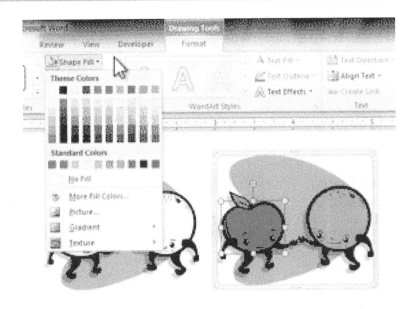

191. Delete and Add Elements

Click on any element to remove, and tap Delete on the keyboard.

To add an element, **create it using INSERT SHAPES and position it in the Drawing Canvas**.

192. Regroup the Image

To finish, **click anywhere inside the Drawing Canvas and SELECT ALL or CTRL-A again. On the DRAWING TOOLS ribbon, click on GROUP, and then on the GROUP option**.

Leave the graphic in the **Drawing Canvas**, or cut and paste it directly back on the page. If I do the latter, I have to be sure to delete the Drawing Canvas when I'm done.

3-D Graphics

I can literally make my text boxes, shapes, and other objects pop off the page by applying a 3-D rotation, bevels, and other 3-dimensional effects to the object. This makes a text box or shape look like it's moving towards the viewer, adding a modern flair.

193. 3-D Rotation

Click on the Text Box, Shape, or Picture. On the DRAWING TOOLS ribbon, click the LAUNCHER BUTTON next to SHAPE STYLES.

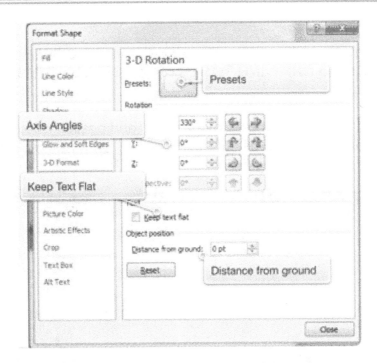

In the **FORMAT SHAPE dialog box, click on 3-D ROTATION on the left. Pick one of the PRESETS as a starting point.**

- **PARALLEL** rotations make shapes that look like parallelograms, where the top & bottom or left & right sides are equal and parallel to each other.
- **PERSPECTIVE** rotations turn the object so that it looks like it's moving to or away from the reader. The top & bottom or left & right sides have one longer than the other.
- **OBLIQUE** effects make cubes. When first applied, there may not be much visible effect until Depth is applied.

In the **ROTATION section, increase and decrease the X, Y, and Z-AXES to spin the object**. Use extreme numbers to flip it backwards or upside down.

A checkmark in front of **KEEP TEXT FLAT** keeps any text within the shape normal, even as the perspective changes. Usually this is left empty.

DISTANCE FROM GROUND moves the object up or down from its starting point.

If the results look completely wonky, and it would be better to start over, **click RESET**. Otherwise, **click CLOSE to save the changes**, or adjust the 3-D Format settings.

194. 3-D Format

3-D Formatting modifies the shape and depth of the object.

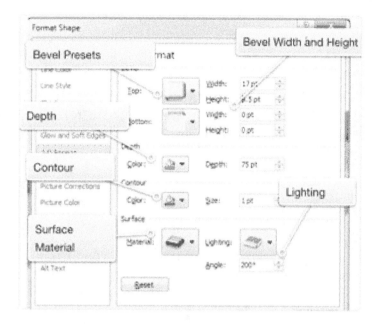

- **BEVEL TOP AND BOTTOM PRESETS** give curves and angles to the edges. Use **TOP or BOTTOM** depending on the object's angle. Use **WIDTH** to adjust how far into the center of the object the effect travels, and **HEIGHT** to determine the depth of the bevels.
- **DEPTH** gives the object dimension—it's the most important of the 3-D effects. The larger the number, the more it pops off the page. Use **COLOR** to change the shading of the object's sides.
- **CONTOUR** places a stroke line at the highlight point of the angle or curve for emphasis. In a box, it's the edges. In a circle, it's where the lighting changes.

SURFACE adjusts the glossiness of the object. Set the **MATERIAL** to control the texture and color. Change the **LIGHTING** to determine the direction and angle of the lighting source.

Gradients

Gradients color an object by gently morphing from one color to another. When using a Gradient as an object fill, I use Word's presets, or adjust the colors to my liking.

195. Using Shape Fill Gradients

Click on any AUTOSHAPE or TEXT BOX. On the DRAWING TOOLS→FORMAT ribbon, click on SHAPE FILL, then hover over GRADIENT. The **LIGHT VARIATIONS** go from a single color to white. The **DARK VARIATIONS** go from a single color to black.

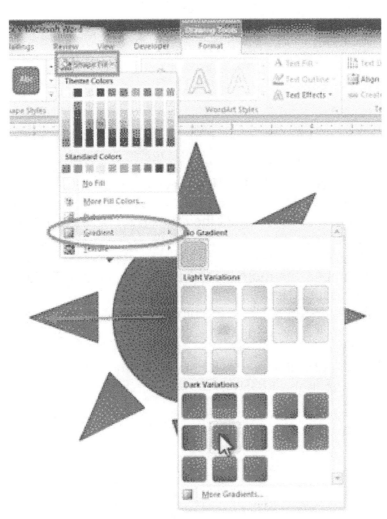

196. More Gradients

At the bottom of that same drop-down menu, **chose MORE GRADIENTS**.... The **FORMAT SHAPE dialog box** is already in the Fill section. **Click on the radio button in front of GRADIENT FILL. Drop down the PRESET COLORS box to pick from a range of attractive multicolor Gradients**. Modify these using the Gradient Stops instructions below.

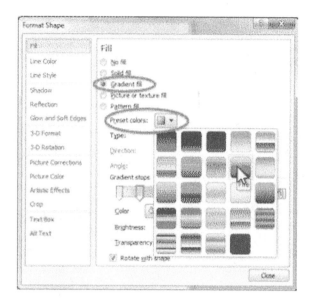

197. Gradient Type and Direction

Use **TYPE** and **DIRECTION** in combination to get the desired look. **Use the TYPE drop-down to select the shape of the Gradient: LINEAR, RADIAL, RECTANGULAR, AND PATH. Drop down the DIRECTION to choose the flow of the colors.**

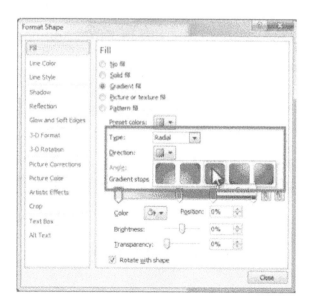

198. Gradient Stops

Use Gradient Stops to adjust the color blend, or the rate of the morphing from one shade to the next.

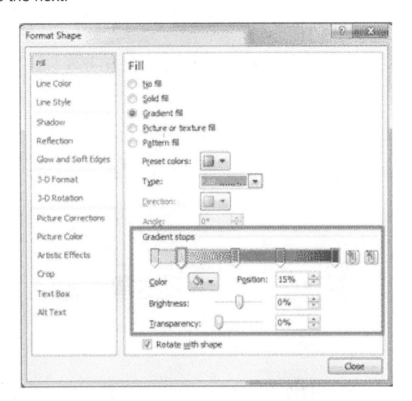

To change a color, click on the arrow, then on the COLOR drop-down. Pick a different color. Use the BRIGHTNESS and TRANSPARENCY sliders to refine each color.

To add a color stop, click on the color bar in a location with no arrow. Use the above adjustments to fine-tune. In the picture to the right, a blue Stop was added between the orange and red.

To delete a STOP, click on it, then look to the right of the color bar and click on the arrow with the red X.

To emphasize different colors, slide the arrows back and forth. Another way is to **click on an arrow and manually change the POSITION: %.**

In the picture to the right, the arrows are slid so that the new blue Gradient Stop doesn't bleed into the center circle.

199. Rotate With Shape

By default, the gradient travels and rotates with the shape, maintaining its current appearance.

Uncheck ROTATE WITH SHAPE to turn and move the shape independently— the gradient stays where it is.

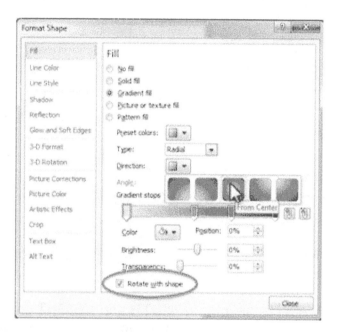

Cropping With Shapes

Who says a picture needs to be rectangular? Turn an image into any shape!

200. Crop to Shape

Insert any picture, and change its **WRAP STYLE to Square or Tight.**

On the PICTURE TOOLS→FORMAT ribbon, click on the CROP drop-down arrow on the far right. Hover over CROP TO SHAPE and choose a Shape to use to mask the image. Choose a relevant Shape carefully—some cut out necessary parts of the image.

201. Format Picture Crop

Once the Shape mask is in place, it's possible to modify the size of the image and the size of the Shape independently.

Click on the PICTURE STYLES LAUNCHER BUTTON, then on the CROP button at the bottom of the list.

PICTURE POSITION affects the image. **WIDTH** and **HEIGHT** change the size dimensions. Note that they do *not* maintain proportions. **OFFSET X** and **OFFSET Y** move the picture left, right, up and down *within* the Shape.

CROP POSITION affects the Shape. **WIDTH** and **HEIGHT** change its dimensions. **LEFT** and **TOP** refer to its distance from the edge of the page.

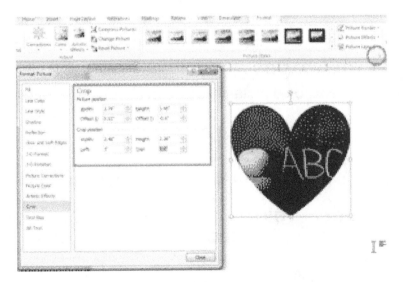

Graphic Size and Location

It's easy to use the Resize Handles to change the size of an object and drag it where you want it. But here are several techniques to give more precision.

202. Using the Keyboard

When dragging a graphic's sizing handles, use the corners to maintain a picture's proportion. Using the handles along the sides can distort an image, making it tall and skinny, or short and fat.

To avoid distortion, **Hold down the SHIFT KEY when clicking-and-dragging, and the height & width adjust together.** Hold down the Shift key when drawing an oval to create a circle. Hold down the Shift key when drawing a rectangle to create a square.

When positioning a graphic, use the ↑, ↓, ←, and → ARROWS on the keyboard to fine-tune the position. For even more precision, hold down the CTRL key to nudge in finer increments. Hold down the ALT key, and the arrows adjust the height and width of the object. Note that this technique may not work depending on your particular keyboard or operating system.

203. Position

On the **PICTURE TOOLS ribbon, use the POSITION button to automatically relocate the image and have text flow around it**. Choices include the nine combinations of **TOP, MIDDLE, BOTTOM, LEFT, CENTER, and RIGHT**.

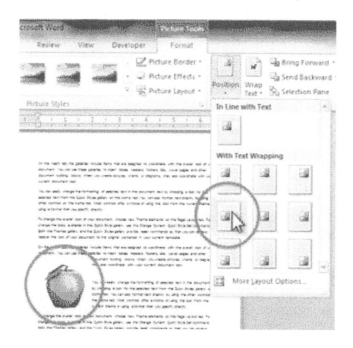

204. Absolute and Relative Height and Width

For precise control over a shape's size, compare it to the proportions of the printed page. For example, I can resize an image to half of the width of the page, or three times wider than the left margin.

Click the LAUNCHER BUTTON under the SIZE group on the far right of the PICTURE TOOLS ribbon. A Layout dialog box opens.

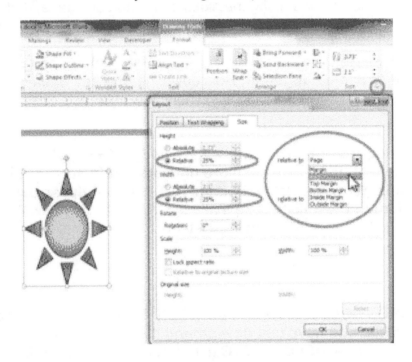

A graphic's real size is its **ABSOLUTE HEIGHT AND WIDTH**. It's measured in inches.

Click on RELATIVE HEIGHT and RELATIVE WIDTH, then use the drop-down to select what the size % will be related to. Choices include the page size and the margins. For example, if I choose 200% relative to one of the Margins, the picture is always twice the Margin size, even if I change it. Note that both Height and Width have to be set separately.

SCALE changes the size by percentage instead of absolute size. For example, I can make it 80% smaller. **Keep LOCK ASPECT RATIO on to change both the Height and Width proportions at the same time.**

Turn on **RELATIVE TO ORIGINAL PICTURE SIZE** to maintain the original dimensions as 100%. If unchecked or the option is grayed out, then when the dialog box is closed, the new size becomes 100% the next time this dialog box is opened. This can be a problem if I later wish to make a picture large again.

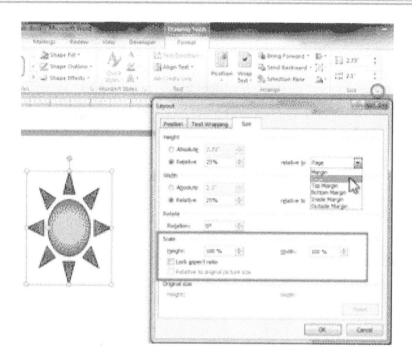

205. Absolute and Relative Position

Use Position to locate a graphic relative to a specific part of the page, even if the margin size, page size, or number of columns changes.

On the **POSITION Tab** in the **LAYOUT** dialog box (or **click the Position button on the ribbon and choose MORE LAYOUT OPTIONS**...), I have many choices for **HORIZONTAL and VERTICAL POSITION**.

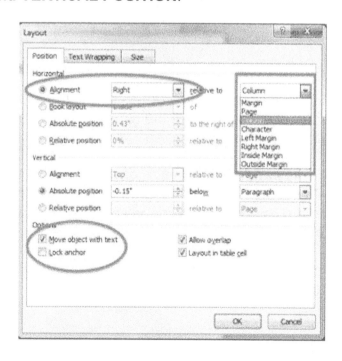

Position	Dimension	Relative To
Alignment	Left, Center, or Right	Margin, Page, Column, or Character
Book Layout	Inside or Outside Edge	Margin or Page
Absolute Position	Inches	To the Right of the Margin, Page, Column, or Character
Relative Position	Percentage	Margin or Page

MOVE OBJECT WITH TEXT keeps the object with the content, even if it shifts.

LOCK ANCHOR prevents me from moving the graphic.

Align, Distribute, and Group

When I have several images that I need to organize on my page, I don't have to align them by eye – Word has extensive tools to arrange the images. In addition, once I've set them perfectly, I like to group them into one large object that I can then move and manipulate with ease, instead of struggling to keep multiple independent graphics united.

206. Align Edges

Click on an image, and dots appear in the corners and in the middle of each side. Not only do these circles or squares resize the dimensions of the object, they can also be used to line up several objects.

Hold down the SHIFT key and click on each of the graphics to line up. On the **PICTURE TOOLS→FORMAT ribbon, click on the ALIGN button and then choose one of the first 6 options**. Each image shows which edge or set of handles can be used for the alignment.

To get two objects perfectly centered, **SHIFT-CLICK on both of them, choose ALIGN CENTER, then ALIGN MIDDLE**.

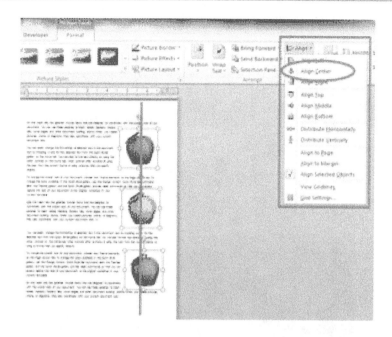

207. Distribute Evenly

When I have three or more graphics that I want to spread evenly across a space, I start by **dragging the first item to its starting location, then dragging the last item to its ending location. Then I'll make sure the middle one is somewhere in-between.**

For example, if I have three objects that I want to spread across the page from top to bottom, I'll drag the first item so its top edge is at the top margin, and the last item so its bottom edge is along the bottom margin.

Now SHIFT-CLICK on all the items. Next, use the ALIGN tools if necessary so that the objects are straight. **Then, click on the ALIGN button again, and choose DISTRIBUTE HORIZONTALLY or DISTRIBUTE VERTICALLY**. All the objects are now spread out so that the spacing is equal between each one.

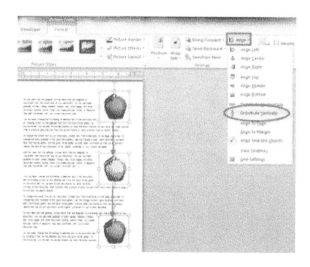

208. Group Multiple Objects into one

Once the objects are lined up and spaced nicely, Group them to maintain and manipulate them as one object instead of several.

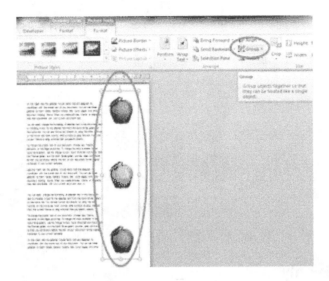

SHIFT-CLICK on each one so they're all selected. On the PICTURE TOOLS→ FORMAT Tab, click on the GROUP button, and choose GROUP.

All the items now have one bounding box. When I move it, all travel together. Even better, if I resize it, all the objects resize proportionally.

Best of all, I can still click on any one item and make color changes.

To separate them again, click on the GROUP button and select UNGROUP.

The Selection and Visibility Pane

When arranging several images so that they overlap, Word has tools to manipulate them as layers on the page.

209. The Selection Pane

Insert one or more of the graphics. **On the PICTURE TOOLS→FORMAT Tab, click on the SELECTION PANE button**. A list of all the graphics on that page appears in the Selection Pane.

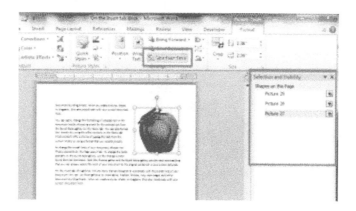

210. Visibility Buttons

Click on the EYE to the right of each graphic to temporarily hide it. This toggle allows me to see objects that are behind other objects. **Click again to show each object**.

At the bottom of the pane are the **SHOW ALL** and **HIDE ALL buttons**.

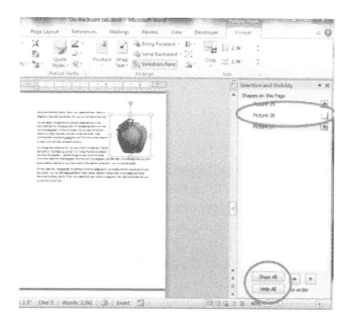

211. Reorder Layers

To change the order of the objects' overlap, **click on one of the graphics, then on the Re-order Up and Down arrows**. The front item is at the top of the list, and the back item on the bottom.

I could always use the **BRING FORWARD** and **SEND BACKWARD** buttons on the ribbon to do my layering, but the **SELECTION AND VISIBILITY PANE** provides a visual representation of the order.

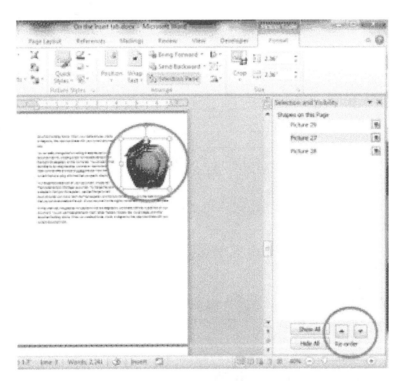

Compress Pictures

Every time an image is inserted into a Word document, the full size of the graphic is added to the file size. For example, if I insert a 2MB picture, my Word document grows by 2MB. When I have a lot of graphics, my file size can become unwieldy. It can make Word slow down, or crash. Plus, it becomes impossible to email the file.

Compressing the images allows me to discard "extra" pixels and keep the file size as small as possible.

If applying Artistic Effects, compress the pictures first so that the quality of the special effects isn't reduced.

212. Compress Pictures

Click on a photograph (compressing doesn't work on Shapes or some Clip Art).
On the PICTURE TOOLS→FORMAT Tab, click on COMPRESS PICTURES.

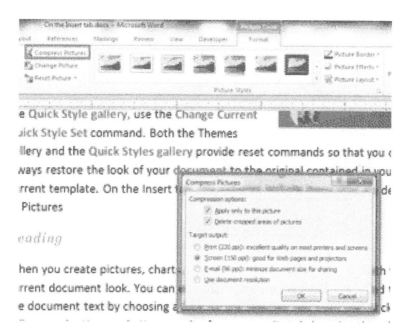

- **APPLY ONLY TO THIS PICTURE** compresses only the active image. If I **UNCHECK the box**, all the graphics are compressed. I do this after my document is finished, otherwise I'll have to do it again later if I add more graphics.
- **DELETE CROPPED AREAS OF PICTURES** completely removes areas of an image that I've **cropped**. This is a great way to remove large areas of the picture completely, but note that it's not possible to Reset a picture to its original state later.
- **TARGET OUTPUT** determines how much compression Word applies. Choose according to the final purpose. **"PPI"** means "pixels per inch." A printer can print more dots than can be seen on the computer screen.
- If the document will be printed, use **PRINT (220 ppi)**, otherwise the graphics will be fuzzy.
- **SCREEN (150 ppi)** is perfect for documents that will be viewed on a computer, or projected onto a screen, but not printed.
- **EMAIL (96 ppi)** creates the smallest file. Large files can't be emailed to some addresses — under 2MB is always safe.
- **USE DOCUMENT RESOLUTION** defaults to the Target Output specified in Word's Options.

213. Compression Defaults

Go to FILE→OPTIONS→ADVANCED→IMAGE SIZE AND QUALITY.

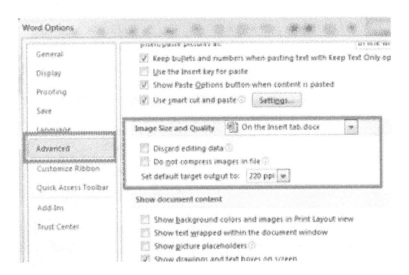

The Compression defaults are applied just to this document only, unless I click on the drop-down and change it to "**ALL NEW DOCUMENTS**."

- **DISCARD EDITING DATA** automatically deletes all the information about the original image, so I won't be able to use the RESET button to start over again. Word permanently "forgets" the original size, color, and crop. To remove any formatting I already applied, I have to delete the image and reinsert it again.
- **DO NOT COMPRESS IMAGES IN FILE** turns off Word's ability to compress the images in the document. This maintains the highest quality, but results in huge file sizes.
- **SET DEFAULT TARGET OUTPUT TO:** allows me to specify whether I want the graphic resolution for all inserted images to be automatically set for Print, Screen, or Email by default.

-

Disable Hardware Graphics Acceleration

One of the innovations in Office 2010 is that it includes Graphics Processing Unit (GPU) acceleration. Word harnesses some of the GPU to make its image effects less draining on your computer.

The system requirements of Office 2010 include a DirectX 9.0c-compatible graphics card with 64 MB or higher video memory. If you're running an older computer, you may get an error message when you try a graphic-intensive feature.

Other symptoms of the inability to use Graphics Acceleration include black or missing images.

If this is happening to you, turn off Word's built-in Hardware Graphics Acceleration option. It's ON by default.

214. Disable Graphics Acceleration

Go to FILE→OPTIONS. Click on ADVANCED.

Scroll down to the DISPLAY section.

Put a checkmark in front of DISABLE HARDWARE GRAPHICS ACCELERATION. Close Word, and start it again.

If there's still a problem, then it's a different issue. Turn the feature back on again.

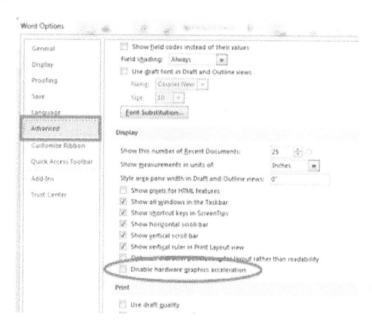

CHAPTER 13: INTEGRATING OFFICE APPLICATIONS

The beauty of Microsoft Office is that it's a suite,
a set of tools that coordinate when managing content.

Here are some Tricks you can use to move content in and out of Word,
using Excel, PowerPoint, and other Word files.

Other Word Files

215. Insert Existing Word Files

When I have an entire Word document that I'd like to insert into a new document, I resist my instinct to open it, select everything, and perform a Copy/Paste.

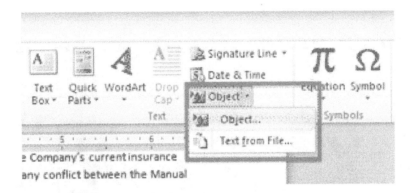

Instead, I follow these steps:

1. **Click where the new content goes.**
2. **Click on the INSERT ribbon.**
3. **Click on the drop-down arrow next to the OBJECT button.**
4. **Click on TEXT FROM FILE…**
5. **Navigate to the file to include, and click INSERT.**
6. **The entire file is now inserted into the document.**

Link to Existing Spreadsheets

Excel spreadsheets can be referenced in a Word document by inserting them as Objects. This way, they can be edited them right in Word, using Excel's tools.

It's also possible to Link to the original so any changes made to it are automatically updated in the destination document.

216. Paste Special

Select and copy data from a spreadsheet. Click in the Word document at the desired location.

On the HOME ribbon, drop down the arrow under the PASTE button, and choose PASTE SPECIAL.

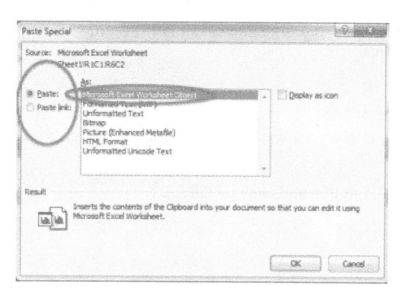

In the window that appears, **click MICROSOFT EXCEL WORKSHEET OBJECT, then click OK**.

The spreadsheet inserts as an object—note the square handles in the corners.

Double-click on it, and it turns into a miniature Excel spreadsheet.

The ribbon temporarily shows Excel tools, until I click off the object and back into my document.

217. Paste Special As Link

The benefit of Paste Link is that changes to the original Excel file are updated every time the document is opened.

This procedure is exactly the same as above, except that in the dialog box, **click on PASTE LINK**.

Now, **when I double-click on the spreadsheet, it opens up the original file in Excel**.

Right-click on the spreadsheet object and select UPDATE LINK to refresh it any time, without opening Excel.

The drawback is that if the original document is moved or renamed (or not emailed along with this file), the spreadsheet turns into a static document.

If the link breaks, **right-click on it and select LINKED WORKSHEET OBJECT** to modify the destination link.

218. Create From File

The second way to insert a linked spreadsheet allows me to do so without opening Excel to cut & paste.

Go to the INSERT ribbon and click on OBJECT.

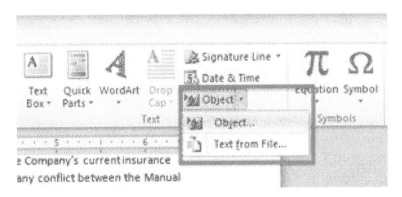

In the dialog box, go to the CREATE FROM FILE Tab. Put a checkmark in front of LINK TO FILE. Browse to the desired spreadsheet.

After I insert it, I can double-click on the object to open the original Excel file, and it works the same way as it did to Paste Special as Link.

Occasionally, I get extra empty cells. If this happens, make sure the cursor is inside the desired range when saving the Excel file. Another possible solution is to SET THE PRINT AREA within the Excel spreadsheet.

219. Update Links Before Printing

Just to make sure the data is up-to-date before committing it to paper, **go to FILE→ OPTIONS→DISPLAY, and scroll down to PRINTING OPTIONS. Put a check in front of UPDATE LINKED DATA BEFORE PRINTING**.

Every time I print, Word updates the Excel file, and all other links, automatically.

Convert An Outline to PowerPoint

If my Word document has been properly formatted using **Heading 1, Heading 2, and Heading 3 styles**, or I've been making good use of the Outline View, I can use my file to create an instant PowerPoint presentation.

There's no need to retype it into PowerPoint, or to copy & paste all the content!

220. Use Heading Styles or Outline View

Set up the Word document so that the content to be the **SLIDE TITLES** is formatted with the **Heading 1 Style**.

Make the BULLETS Heading 2 Style.

Make SUB-BULLETS Heading 3, 4, and 5 Styles.

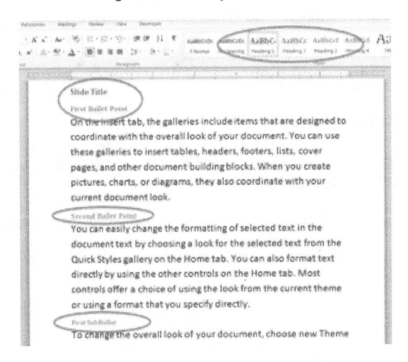

Any other "body text" content not in these three styles will be ignored in the PowerPoint conversion.

Look at the document using **OUTLINE VIEW**, and see **+ signs** to the left of text indicating that it will appear in the slideshow. **BODY TEXT** with a **Circle** in front of it will be ignored.

Delete any **EXTRA BLANK LINES** that are formatted as **Headings**, or they will become slides!

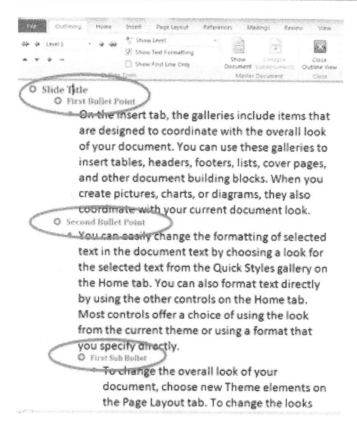

221. Import Slides From Outline

In a blank PowerPoint slideshow, **click on the drop-down below NEW SLIDE. Choose SLIDES FROM OUTLINE.... Navigate to the target Word file and open it.**

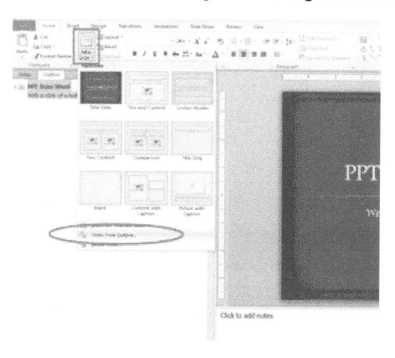

222. Use Outline View in PowerPoint
Switch from Slide View to OUTLINE VIEW.

My Heading 1 Styles are now slides. My Heading 2 Styles are now bullets. My Heading 3 Styles are now sub-bullets. Any Heading 4 and 5 Styles are indented under that.

Sometimes the converted content doesn't come across exactly right. **Click on the errant text and PROMOTE or DEMOTE the content to the correct indent levels.**

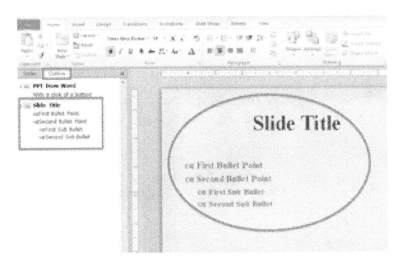

CHAPTER 14: WHAT'S NEXT

Did you learn anything?

Still hungry for more?

Here are some additional resources you can use to become a master, and get your questions answered.

Royalwise Solutions, Inc.

Royalwise Solutions, Inc. is Portland, Oregon's premier resource for training in Microsoft Office, Apple products, and Intuit's QuickBooks and Quicken.

Here's how we can be of service:

Textbooks

This book is also available as a multi-touch book with interactive image galleries and a demo movie. Check it out in the **iTunes Store**!

Personal Training

Alicia is for hire! **Do you just need an hour of time** to have a few questions answered about a project you're working on?

We can work together over iChat/Messages, Skype, JoinMe, or other screen sharing software to **train you right on your own computer**, no matter where you live. Don't worry, we'll help get you set up for screen sharing!

Corporate Training

Do you have a business with employees who need training? We can help, even if you live outside the Portland, OR area.

Email Newsletter

We send out periodic emails featuring Apple support and training. If you have a Mac, iPhone, or iPad, we'll help you use your equipment to their fullest capabilities. **Sign up at http://www.royalwise.com/.**

YouTube

Alicia's **"GetTheMaxFromYourMac" YouTube channel** features useful how-to videos about Microsoft Office and Mac OSX.

Facebook

LIKE Royalwise Solutions on Facebook to receive tips and advice in your Newsfeed.

Twitter

Follow @royalwise to have our articles pop up in your stream.

Lynda.com

Alicia Katz Pollock is an author at http://www.lynda.com/AliciaKatzPollock, an online video training portal with over 1,500 courses about all kinds of computer software and photography.

The Word 2010 Tips & Tricks in this book are performed live by Alicia as training videos at **http://www.lynda.com/AliciaKatzPollock**.

As our gift to you, here's a link to a free 7-day trial: **http://www.lynda.com/trial/apollock**.

Join Alicia for additional Microsoft Office courses in:

- **PowerPoint 2010 Power Shortcuts**—Learn 50 Tips & Tricks to make PowerPoint quicker, easier, and more powerful so you can create better slideshows.
- **PowerPoint 2010 Audio & Video In Depth**—Learn everything there is to know about inserting movies and sound into PowerPoint 2010 presentations.
- **PowerPoint 2007 Audio & Video In Depth**—Learn everything there is to know about inserting movies and sound into PowerPoint 2007 presentations.
- **Outlook for Mac 2011 Essential Training**—Alicia covers all the features of Outlook for Mac to get you up and running.
- **Access 2010 Essential Training**—Build your own database from scratch using these lessons on creating Tables, Forms, Queries, Reports, and Macros.
- **Access 2010 Power Shortcuts**—100 Tips & Tricks you can use to make Access 2010 more efficient and powerful.
- **What's New in Access 2010**—If you're upgrading from Access 2007 or 2003, here's what you need to know.
- **Access 2007 Power Shortcuts**—100 Tips & Tricks you can use to make Access 2007 more efficient and powerful.

INDEX

About the Author

Alicia Katz Pollock is the President of **Royalwise Solutions, Inc.**.

When she was 13, Alicia received her first computer, an Apple IIc. She immediately designed a database for her father's dental practice to automatically send postcards to his patients every 6 months to come in for a checkup and cleaning. Her passion for computers grew as she did.

A natural teacher, Alicia earned her Master of Arts in Teaching from Tufts University, but instead of turning to the public schools, she developed computer curricula.

She blends the skills of technology, the art of communication, the patience of a trainer, the wisdom of a business consultant, and the detailed eye of an obsessive/compulsive to bring you the finest in business solutions.

Alicia has held **Microsoft Office Specialist certifications** at the Master level since 1992.

She has authored many courses in Microsoft Word, PowerPoint, Access, and Outlook for **Lynda.com**.

She is a member of the **Apple Consultants Network**.

She is an **Intuit ProAdvisor**.

She taught Microsoft Office at Heald College and Corinthian (Western Business) College.

Read our blog and sign up for our newsletter: **http://royalwise.com/**

Follow us on Facebook: **http://www.facebook.com/RoyalwiseSolutions**

Follow us on Twitter: **http://www.twitter.com/royalwise**

This book is also available as a searchable eBook at Smashwords, **https://www.smashwords.com/books/view/330752?ref=royalwise**, and as a multi-touch Apple iBook with interactive image galleries and a demo movie. Check it out in the **iTunes Store: http://tinyurl.com/n37uko9**.

www.ingramcontent.com/pod-product-compliance
Lightning Source LLC
Chambersburg PA
CBHW080409060326
40689CB00019B/4183